DONALD W. TREADGOLD STUDIES
ON
RUSSIA, EAST EUROPE, AND CENTRAL ASIA

The Editor of Treadgold Studies is Glennys Young,
Associate Professor of History and International Studies,
University of Washington.

From 1994 to 2001, the Editor of Treadgold Papers
was Professor Sabrina Ramet.

Books in the Treadgold Studies series honor the memory
and distinguished contributions of Donald W. Treadgold,
who taught Russian history at the
University of Washington from 1949 to 1993.

Perils of Pankratova
Some Stories from the Annals of Soviet Historiography. 2005.
Reginald E. Zelnik

Plays of Expectations
Intertextual Relations in Russian Twentieth-Century Drama. 2006.
Andrew Baruch Wachtel

War in a European Borderland
Occupations and Occupation Plans in Galicia and Ukraine, 1914–1918.
2007.
Mark von Hagen

WAR IN A EUROPEAN BORDERLAND

Occupations and Occupation Plans in Galicia and Ukraine, 1914–1918

Mark von Hagen

Published by the Herbert J. Ellison Center for Russian,
East European, and Central Asian Studies, University of Washington

Distributed by the University of Washington Press
Seattle and London

Printed in the United States of America
12 11 10 09 08 07 06   5 4 3 2 1

Russian, East European, and Central Asian Studies Center (REECAS)
Henry M. Jackson School of International Studies, University of Washington
www.depts.washington.edu/reecas
For more information about the Treadgold Series and previously published Treadgold Papers, visit www.jsis.washington/edu/ellison/outreach_treadgold.shtml

University of Washington Press
P.O. Box 50096, Seattle, WA 98145-5096
www.washington.edu/uwpress

Library of Congress Cataloging-in-Publication Data
Von Hagen, Mark, 1954–
War in a European borderland : occupations and occupation plans in Galicia and Ukraine, 1914–1918 / Mark von Hagen.
p. cm. — (Donald W. Treadgold studies on Russia, East Europe, and Central Asia)
Includes bibliographical references.
ISBN-13: 978-0-295-98753-8 (pbk. : alk. paper)
ISBN-10: 0-295-98753-7 (pbk. : alk. paper)
1. World War, 1914–1918—Galicia (Poland and Ukraine) 2. World War, 1914–1918—Ukraine. 3. Galicia (Poland and Ukraine)—History—20th century. 4. Ukraine—History—20th century. I. Title.
D623.U38V66   2007
940.4'147—dc22   2007030286

CONTENTS

PREFACE and ACKNOWLEDGMENTS

For a historian of armies and soldiers such as myself, Ukraine has an obvious if morbid attraction as a veritable battleground for invading armies from diverse directions and in changing historical circumstances, most often in modern history from Russia and Germany, but also from Poland, Austria-Hungary, and Napoleonic France. (During the Civil War that followed on the world war that is the focus of this volume, troops from Britain and France joined the Reds, Whites, Greens, and Poles in attempts to claim Ukraine's territory, population, and resources for their imperial, national, or internationalist ambitions.) But the character of Ukraine as a combat zone and invasion path has been reflected, not surprisingly, in a fierce historiographic rivalry over Ukraine as well. Several competing Ukrainian narratives in turn set themselves against Russian, Polish, and Jewish variants of the past, with each of these, too, divided among several rival schools of interpretation. The primary narratives are unfolded to various degrees in the German, Austrian, and North American histories that build on them.[1]

About a dozen years ago, then, I embarked on what I came to half-jokingly refer to as my "self-Ukrainianization." The result was that, from feeling inadequate as a historian of the Russian Empire and the Soviet Union because of my lack of familiarity with the histories of the peoples who have historically constituted those two state formations, I went to feeling myself a very inadequate historian of Ukraine. I committed myself to learning what I quickly came to realize was a whole new field; and I owe much to my teachers in that field, most of whom I count as friends although a few died before I had the opportunity to make their acquaintance: Olga Andriewsky, John Armstrong, John-Paul Himka, Yaroslav Hrytsak, Taras Hunczak, Zenon Kohut, Ivan Lysiak-Rudnytsky, Robert Paul Magocsi, Alexander Motyl, Yaroslav Pelensky, Serhii Plokhii, Anna Procyk, Marc Raeff, Orest Subtelny, Frank Sysyn, Roman Szporluk, Stephen Velychenko, Vladyslav Verstiuk, and many others whose works will be gratefully cited in the footnotes in the succeeding chapters. Along the way I also met Andreas Kappeler and Hans-Joachim Torke, who came to Ukrainian history from somewhat different directions than my own but who shared many of my "coming from the outsider" perspectives and—perhaps—shortcomings in the eyes of some of our colleagues. I am also grateful to several non-

Ukrainian specialists whose work on World War I has enlivened our discussions of late imperial Russia: Peter Gatrell, Peter Holquist, and Eric Lohr, to name only a few, together with the patient and generous audiences with whom I shared earlier versions of this work in Palo Alto, Seattle, New York, Burlington, and Slavs'ke (Ukraine). All these scholars will recognize large chunks of their wisdom pirated for my own purposes, but I very much hope that I can repay my debt to them by adding something new to the story of Ukraine in the way that I frame that story and with the archival work that I bring to the core time period of this study. Still, I suspect that these colleagues might disagree occasionally not only with minor matters of interpretation but very likely with some of the larger frameworks in which I set that story and the intellectual and historiographical consequences that flow from those choices.

The best of my colleagues in the Ukrainian history field are almost instinctively comparativists and transnationalists because of the subject matter at the center of our fascination. Most obviously, they place the history of Ukraine in its broader central and east European contexts. Russia is often an unspoken comparison as is Poland; the social structures and political-cultural opportunities of Ukrainians in the Russian Empire are contrasted with those in the Austro-Hungarian lands; and later the host/occupier states are Poland and the Soviet Union. The period I have chosen to organize this volume, 1914–1918, also explores the continuities and differences between the place of Ukraine in the Russian Empire and in Austria-Hungary. Insisting on the multicultural character of modern Ukraine, I also sporadically, but inadequately, compare the Ukrainian national movements with their Polish, Russian, and Jewish counterparts, as well as with political movements based on class or other unifying principles.[2]

I buttressed this set of intellectual orientations toward comparison and alternative-seeking by an archival research strategy that opened multiperspectival windows on my subject. I worked in Russia (RGVIA, the Russian State Military-History Archive; RGVA, the Russian State Military Archive; and RTsKhIDNI), Ukraine (party and state), Canada (National Archive), Germany (Militaer-Archiv), Poland (Centralne Archiwum Wojskowe and Archiwum Wschodnie), and the United States (Hoover Institution at Stanford and Bakhmeteff Collections at Columbia University) in an effort to look at my object from as many points as I could manage. I thank all the archivists and other scholars who guided me through the archives: Hennady Boriak, Liudmilla Dvoinykh, Viktor Filatov, Irina Garkusha, Alexander Kavtaradze, Vera Mikhaleva, Myron Momryk, Albert Nenarokov, Ruslan Pyrih, Mikhail Ryzhenkov; and Nonna Tarkhova. Several endowments have helped to materially support this long reeducation process: the Alexander von Humboldt Foundation (Germany), the National Endowment for the Humanities, the Social Science Research Council, the Ford Foundation, the Ukrainian Studies Fund, the Petro Jacyk Foundation, the Shevchenko Scientific Society, the Ukrainian Academy of Arts and Science in America, the Canadian Institute of Ukrainian Studies, the Open Society Institute, and others. Ron Meyer at the Harriman Institute has been a wonderful editor and friend over the years; he saw through a final reading of this manuscript and helped make the text a better one.

Finally, my interest in World War I took me back to my own family history, in which my paternal grandfather, Leo Von Hagen, a German-American, fought in France but to his dying day could not understand what possessed the American leadership to involve our country in this absurd European family feud; and to my maternal great-grandfather, Maximilian Koenig, who fought in the army of Emperor Francis Joseph on the Italian front. It is to these two ancestors and their families who lived through the war that I dedicate this book.

My intention was to offer—as much as possible—a stereoscopic view of events and processes, while acknowledging that, for purposes of narrative coherence, I somehow had to center the story, although allowing that center to shift from chapter to chapter. It will be up to the reader to judge the success of those efforts.

Mark von Hagen
New York City
February 2007

NOTES

1. See Robert Paul Magocsi, *A History of Ukraine* (Seattle, WA: University of Washington Press, 1996), chapter 2 ("Historical Perceptions") for a very lucid statement of the issues at stake; see also Stephen Velychenko, *National History as Cultural Process: A Survey of the Interpretations of Ukraine's Past in Polish, Russian, and Ukrainian Historical Writing from Earliest Times to 1914* (Edmonton, AB: Canadian Institute of Ukrainian Studies Press, 1992); and his *Shaping Identity in Eastern Europe and Russia: Soviet-Russian and Polish Accounts of Ukrainian History, 1914–1991* (New York: St. Martin's Press, 1993). For a brief introduction to German-language historiography, see Andreas Kappeler, "Die Ukraine in der deutschsprachigen Historiographie," in *Ukraine*, ed. Peter Jordan, Andreas Kappeler, Walter Lukan, and Josef Vogl (Vienna: Peter Lang, 2000), pp. 161–179.
2. I have also benefited from team teaching with colleagues at Columbia University who have enhanced my comparativist perspective on Ukraine's history: Michael Stanislawski (Russian and East European Jewish history), Richard Wortman (Imperial Russia), and Karen Barkey (Ottoman history). In addition, I have learned a great deal from colleagues in several summer school and conference/workshop settings: Anatoly Remnev (Omsk), Boris Anan'ich (St. Petersburg), Rafail Ganelin (St. Petersburg), Petr Savel'ev (Samara), Yaroslav Hrytsak (L'viv), Aleksei Miller (Moscow/Budapest), and Jane Burbank (New York University, earlier University of Michigan).

NOTE ON TRANSLITERATION

Because one of my intentions in this work has been to highlight the different perspectives that succeeding occupation regimes brought to the region, I felt it important to preserve something of the language in which the participants talked about Ukraine and its cities. Instead of the standard contemporary Ukrainian transliteration of all cities located in today's Ukraine, I have rendered the cities in the languages of the occupation regime; hence, during the Russian occupation of 1914–15, L'vov is the designation for the capital of Galicia; during the German occupations, the capital city is Kiew/Kyiv, since the occupiers were dealing with Ukrainian national governments that insisted on the importance of the Ukrainian language. This unorthodox transliteration applies only to place names; I have not tried to do the same for personal names, choosing only one "nationality" for each character in my story.

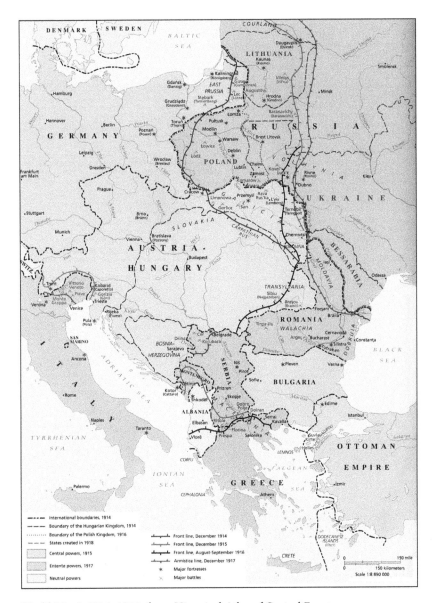

World War I, 1914–1918, from *Historical Atlas of Central Europe*
by Paul Robert Magocsi (Seattle: University of Washington Press, 2002)

WAR IN A EUROPEAN BORDERLAND
Occupations and Occupation Plans in Galicia and Ukraine, 1914–1918

INTRODUCTION

THE HISTORY OF OCCUPATIONS, particularly repeated occupations of one region by neighboring multinational states, provides a rich entry into a study of the way warring powers are forced constantly to reevaluate their wartime aims, their postwar plans, and their domestic and foreign policies in the face of the military and civilian "realities" on the ground. The borderlands that had once been Austrian Ukraine (eastern Galicia and Bukovyna) and Russian Ukraine (Left- and Right-Bank) were subjected during different periods over a relatively short span of time to very intrusive and destructive experiments at projecting the institutional and ideological norms of several states: Austria-Hungary, Germany, the Russian Empire, the Provisional Government, and the Bolshevik Sovnarkom (Council of People's Commissariats). In nearly all cases, large numbers of the Imperial minority populations—including Poles, Jews, Ukrainians, Belorussians, and the Baltic peoples—were fighting on both sides of the war and suffered numerous consequences from the conflicts over their loyalties.[1] Wartime policies in these borderlands exacerbated ethnic tensions by targeting specific national communities. Discriminatory legislation and military commands on both sides privileged or disadvantaged one ethnic group over another in matters of property holding, language, schooling, and religious practice. Still, in large measure, the occupation regimes were attempts to extend the imperial models of the invading power to the territory of its rivals. Importantly, the regimes were shaped by the official war aims of the belligerent powers and by the ways in which those war aims were translated into propaganda for the troops. But the regimes were also the product of the intersection of the occupying authorities with local politics and society, whose prewar dynamics were quickly transformed with the outbreak of war.

The years covered in this study are from the outbreak of the war in July 1914 to the capitulation of the Central Powers in November 1918. The story of occupations in Ukraine, of course, did not conclude with the end of World War I, but continued with Bolshevik, White Army, and Polish regimes until the Treaty of Riga once again divided the Ukrainian population between two states, the Polish Republic and the Soviet Union. For the years 1914–1918, the key periods treated are as follows: (1) Austrian rule in Galicia and Bukovyna until September 1914; (2) Russian occupation of

Galicia and Bukovyna, September 1914–June 1915; (3) German-Austrian reoccupation of Galicia and Bukovyna, plus the Russian provinces of Volynia and Kholm, June 1915–June 1916; (4) second Russian occupation of Galicia and Bukovyna, recovery of lost Russian territories, June 1916–January 1918, with the complication of a regime change in February 1917 from imperial Russia to the Provisional Government and the rise of the Ukrainian Central Rada in Kyiv—including a brief Russian Bolshevik effort to overthrow the Kyiv Rada government that was temporarily successful, but cut short by the German-Austrian agreement to protect the Rada government in the terms of the Brest-Litovsk Peace; and (5) the second German-Austrian occupation of most of Russian Ukraine (and recovery of Austrian Ukraine), including the capital city of Kyiv and the southern provinces of New Russia and Crimea, March–November 1918.

Ukraine and Ukrainians between Two Empires

The focus of this study is the territory and populations claimed at various times during the early twentieth century by the Ukrainian national movement. At the outbreak of the First World War in 1914, those territories and populations were divided between the two empires of the Romanovs and Habsburgs. Austria-Hungary was a constitutional monarchy that granted considerable rights and autonomy to its minority nationalities in what was understood as a *Nationalitaetenstaat*, or state of nationalities. Ukrainians, or Ruthenians as they were identified officially in Austrian documents, elected representatives to the national parliament in Vienna, the *Reichsrat*, and to the local Galician diet, or *sejm*, in Lemberg. Austrian Ukrainians maintained schools in their native Ukrainian language, as well as newspapers and a wide range of other cultural and political associations. They were overwhelmingly Christians, but were divided between the Greek Catholic, or Uniate, Church, with its metropolitan in Lemberg, and the Orthodox Church, with its seat in Czernowitz, the major city of Bukovyna. Austrian Ukrainians were also divided politically into Ukrainophile and Russophile movements, the latter favoring closer ties to Russia, the Russian language, and the Russian Orthodox Church. Although eastern Galicia will be the major actor for Austria-Hungary in this book, Bukovyna is also important and awaits further study. While much of the history to follow was similar in both Ukrainian regions, important regional differences nevertheless shaped different occupation regimes in the two Austrian territories.[2]

4

By 1914 Russia, too, was a constitutional monarchy of sorts, but of very recent origin (1906) and with a host of qualifications, above all a reigning monarch who did his utmost to roll back the concessions to popular sovereignty that imperial society had forced on him in the revolution of 1905. Although Ukrainians in the Russian Empire elected deputies to the first two Dumas, an electoral coup d'état by the government rendered the Duma not representative of the Empire's nationalities and privileged the Russian national parties at the expense of others, including Ukrainians. The Ukrainian language had been banned for most of the second half of the nineteenth century, but the ban had been lifted in 1906 and then partially restored in subsequent years. Although the Ukrainian movement was able to take some advantage of the semi-constitutional regime, the Russian nationalist parties and movements that emerged in opposition to the demands of minority nationalities were much more successful in pushing their counterrevolution. The Russian movements had their origins in the Great Russian nation-building project of the mid-nineteenth century that asserted the primacy of Russian ethnicity, language, and culture in the empire.[3] In short, opportunities for the Ukrainian movement were far better in Austria-Hungary than in Russia; consequently, many Ukrainian activists had abandoned Russia for Galicia to pursue their cause from what became known as the Ukrainian Piedmont. The territories of the Russian Empire at the center of this essay are traditionally known as Left- and Right-Bank Ukraine, and include the important governor-generalship of Kiev/Kyiv (including Poltava and Chernigov/Chernihiv), as well as the provinces of Khar'kov/Kharkiv and Slobozhanshchyna.

In both empires, Ukrainians faced major political and economic rivalry from Poles, but with different imperial arrangements. The Austrians had turned over the key posts in local government in Galicia to the Polish elites, who also viewed the province as a Polish Piedmont intended to recover the nation that had been removed from the map of Europe by the late-eighteenth-century partitions. Russian imperial authorities, by contrast, distrusted the Poles in their southwestern provinces and suspected them, as Roman Catholics, of trying to undermine the various Russian nation-building projects that were being undertaken in the early twentieth century. Those authorities viewed the Ukrainian movement as an artificial invention of the Poles' secessionist ambitions and saw Russian Poles as linked to their Austrian counterparts in perfidious conspiracies.

On the Eve of War in Austrian Ukraine

In the relatively liberal political climate of late imperial Austria-Hungary, Poles and Ruthenians (the Austrian empire's preferred designation for the non-Polish Slavic inhabitants of Galicia and Bukovyna) formed diverse political parties and public organizations that offered different possibilities for expressing ethnonational and religious identities and related geopolitical orientations between Russia and Austria. The Austrian authorities were most concerned by the emergence of a pro-Russian orientation—one that favored the Russian language and Orthodox faith—among their subject populations, and tried to combat it with support for the more loyalist, largely Greek-Catholic or Uniate movement, though this support was tempered by Vienna's reliance on local Poles to administer the provinces. These rivalries were important indicators and catalysts in the changes that the inhabitants of the region would experience before and after 1914. In many ways, these rivalries also shaped the subsequent occupation policies of both the Russian Empire and the Austro-German alliance.

For the Austrians, the major political threat in the immediate prewar years was the Russophile movement and the growing involvement of Russian official and semi-official activists, including their financial backing, in Galician and Bukovynan society.[4] The intellectual origins of the nineteenth-century political movement alternately known as Moscophilism or Russophilism can be traced to the ideas of all-Russian unity developed by the Moscow historian Mikhail Pogodin. Pogodin also made the first research trips to Galicia to agitate among the local population for the political unity of Galician Ukrainians with Russia. The "Old Ruthenian" movement took up these Slavophile ideas and founded institutions—the people's houses (*narodni domy*), the Kachkovskii Society, and the Stauropigianic Institute—to educate young and old among the Slavic populations of Austria-Hungary.[5] The Ukrainophiles responded with their own institutions, notably the *Prosvita* (enlightenment) branches with reading rooms and literacy classes. The competition between Ukrainophiles and Russophiles persisted right up to the outbreak of World War I, though that rivalry would turn deadly on both sides of the imperial borders.

Austrian authorities tolerated this pro-Russian orientation among a significant part of the country's Ruthenian population largely because the Polish elites who governed Galicia for Vienna deemed the Russophiles less of a threat to Polish national aspirations than the emerging parallel

Ukrainophile nationalism. The Russophiles had been encouraged in Austrian Galicia by a series of Polish viceroys, especially Andrzej Potocki and Michal Bobrzynski. This instance of a tactical Polish-Russian union was directed against the Ukrainian national movement, despite the hostility of mainstream Russian nationalism to both the Polish and Ukrainian causes in the Russian Empire itself. Russophiles elected deputies to both the local diet and the imperial parliament in Vienna, including Vladimir Dudykevich and Dmitrii Markov. Both these men had extensive ties with Russian activists, Count Vladimir Bobrinskii, General Vladimirov, and two prominent Orthodox bishops, Evlogii and Antonii, who arranged for generous financial subsidies for the pro-Russian parties' journals and activities. These inter-parliamentary contacts on the eve of the war shared an agenda of broadening the use of the Russian language and the influence of the Orthodox Church in the region; they combated the widespread use of Ukrainian (Ruthenian) and the Greek-Catholic influence.[6]

On the way home from a Slavic Congress that had convened in Prague in 1908, Bobrinskii, Vladimirov, and other Russophiles stopped off in Warsaw, Cracow, Lemberg, and Czernowitz, where they were received triumphantly by local Polish and Russophile activists. On the eve of the war, such visits from Russia became more frequent, as did return visits by Galician delegations to Moscow and St. Petersburg. The collaboration of these two branches of the Russophile movement—one operating in Austria-Hungary and the other in the Russian Empire—gave rise to a cross-border politico-philanthropic association, the Galician-Russian Society (*Galitsko-russkoe obshchestvo*). The society offered Russian language instruction, Orthodox religion, and Russian history, and also supported newspapers. Their geopolitical line was irredentist, and they pledged that, in the event of war between the Habsburg monarchy and Russia, they would fight for the Russian cause. They appealed to the Ruthenian population to turn their weapons not on their "brother Russian soldiers," but instead against their "Swabian" officers to free themselves from the Austrian yoke. Orthodox priests trained in the seminaries of Zhitomir, Kholm, and Kiev were encouraged to return to Galicia and Bukovyna to spread the "Russian" idea. The Russophile priests organized joint pilgrimages to such important monasteries as Pochaev that brought together Russian students and Ukrainian peasants to persuade the two communities of their common interests and identities. (The same sense of wartime possibilities encouraged the Ukrainophiles in Galicia to entertain hopes for a reverse annexation, in which Little Russia would be detached from the Russian Empire and "reunited" with Galicia and Bukovyna. Following Russia's defeat at the hands of Japan in the war of 1904–05, its enemies took heart at the weakness of the tsarist colossus.)

As the war approached, such blatant appeals to deliver Galicia to the Russian emperor and to plant the Russian flag in the Carpathians roused the attention of the local police and military authorities. Not surprisingly, the local authorities began to take measures to shut down the schools and newspapers, censored those publications that were allowed to remain open, and began keeping lists of politically suspect activists. The latter were identified by their frequent trips to Russia, their subscriptions to Russian newspapers, and their support for the Imperial diet candidate Dmitrii Markov. Local authorities' anxieties were fed by the Russophiles' protagonists in the sessions of the *Reichsrat*, who raised fundamental doubts about their rivals' loyalty to the Habsburg throne. Kost' Levyts'kyi, the deputy from Galicia to Vienna, earned a reputation as the "Russophile hunter" for his persistent efforts to draw attention to the growing danger of the Russophile movement. The rise of "spymania" led to the arrest of hundreds of Russophile activists (priests, lawyers, schoolteachers, and others) and the mounting of two very public trials in 1912 and 1914. A third trial planned in Czernowitz failed to take place, despite extensive preparations.[7]

The rise in Russophile activity during the prewar years was largely a reaction to heightened activism from the rival camp claiming the loyalties of the Ruthenian population, the Ukrainophiles. They had assumed the dominant role in Ukrainian politics since the late nineteenth century; local Galician and Bukovynan activists were reinforced by the arrival of dozens of expatriates from the Russian Empire, many of whom became founding members of the Union for the Liberation of Ukraine (ULU). Although members of the ULU were from the left end of the political spectrum—socialists and revolutionaries—they found some common ground with more conservative forces in promoting Ukrainian interests. Metropolitan Andrei Sheptits'kyi, head of the Greek Catholic Church, and the Galician Ukrainian deputies to the Vienna parliament, Kost' Levytsky and Mykola Vasylko, favored a Ukrainian solution tied to Austria-Hungary and encouraged the imperial authorities to keep a watchful eye on the activities of the Russophiles and their Russian patrons.[8] On the very eve of the war, the ULU declared that it would encourage all Ukrainians to fight on the side of the Habsburg emperor against Russia and proposed arming Ukrainians in a separate legion of volunteers.

INTRODUCTION

NOTES

1. For example, Karl Tiander estimated that nearly eight million Poles were fighting for the Central Powers, while another two million were serving in the Russian Army. See his *Das Erwachen Osteuropas. Die Nationalitaetenbewegung in Russland und der Weltkrieg* (Wien-Leipzig: Wilhelm Braumueller, 1934), p.137. Ingeborg Fleischhauer estimates that well over 300,000 ethnic Germans served in the tsar's army against their co-religionists and co-nationals on the German and Austrian side. See *Die Deutschen im Zarenreich: Zwei Jahrhunderte deutsch-russische Kulturgemeinschaft* (Stuttgart: Deutsche Verlags-Anstalt, 1986), p. 461. Heinz-Dietrich Loewe, in *Antisemitismus und reaktionaere Utopie*, estimates that nearly one-tenth of the Jewish population, or about 500,000 Jewish soldiers, fought in the ranks of the Russian Army (p. 146).
2. For a brief but comprehensive survey of Austrian Ukraine in the nineteenth and early twentieth centuries, see Ivan L. Rudnytsky, "The Ukrainians in Galicia under Austrian Rule," in Ivan L. Rudnytsky, *Essays in Modern History* (Edmonton, AB: Canadian Institute of Ukrainian Studies, 1987), pp. 315–352.
3. See Alexei Miller, *"Ukrainskii vopros" v politike vlastei i russkom obshchestvennom mnenii (vtoraia polovina XIX v.)* (St. Petersburg: Aleteia, 2000), esp. pp. 31–45.
4. For a good, recent treatment of Russophilism, see Anna Veronika Wendland, *Die Russophilen in Galizien. Ukrainische Konservative zwischen Oesterreich und Russland 1848–1915* (Wien: Verlag der Österreichischen Akademie der Wissenschaften, 2001). See also Paul Robert Magocsi, "Old Ruthenianism and Russophilism: A New Conceptual Framework for analyzing National Ideologies in Late Nineteenth Century Eastern Galicia," in Paul Debreczeny, ed., *American Contributions to the Ninth International Congress of Slavists*, vol. II (Columbus, OH: Slavica, 1983), 305–324.
5. In addition to the Kachkovskii Society, the Russophiles sponsored a youth organization, *Drug*, a women's organization, *Zhizn'*, and the newspapers, *Prikarpatskaia Rus', Golos naroda, Stavropihiia,* and *Narodnii Dim*.
6. On the efforts of the Orthodox Church to combat the "Ukrainian" idea, see Ricarda Vulpius, *Nationalisierung der Religion: Russifizierungspolitik und ukrainische Nationsbildung 1860–1920* (Wiesbaden: Harrassowitz Verlag, 2005), esp. chapter IV. For Evlogii's prewar activities in the Ukrainian-Russian-Polish borderlands, see Evlogii, Georgievskii (Metropolit), *Put' moei zhizni 1868–1946 Vospominaniia*, ed. T. Manuchina (Paris: YMCA Press, 1947).
7. On the tense atmosphere on the eve of war, see Klaus Bachmann, *"Ein Herd der Feindschaft gegen Russland": Galizien als Krisenherd in den Beziehungen der Donaumonarchie mit Russland (1907–1914)* (Munich: R. Oldenbourg Verlag, 2001), esp. chapter 3.
8. On Ukrainian political life in Galicia, see Kost' Levyts'kyi, *Istoriia politychnoi dumky halyts'kykh ukraintsiv 1848–1914*, 2 vols. (L'viv: p.a.), 1926). On the crucial role of the Greek Catholic Church and clergy in the Ukrainian movement, see John-Paul Himka, "The Greek Catholic Church and Nation-Building in Galicia, 1772–1918," *Harvard Ukrainian Studies*, December 1984, vol. 8, pp. 426–452; and his *Religion and Nationality in Western Ukraine. The Greek Catholic Church and the Ruthenian National Movement in Galicia* (Montreal, QC: McGill-Queen's University Press, 1999).

CHAPTER 1

Outbreak of War and the Transformation of Austrian Galicia

THESE KEY RIVALRIES IN EASTERN GALICIA, between Ukrainophiles and Russophiles, complicated by the rival Polish political parties and orientations, shaped the subsequent occupation policies of both the Russian Empire and the Austro-German alliance. But even before the first Russian occupation in September 1914, the Austrian authorities quickly enacted measures that began to resemble a wartime occupation regime: severe restrictions on political life and public institutions, increased surveillance and arrests of suspected individuals and population groups, even abuses and the first charges of atrocities against the Central Powers. Parliamentary life quieted down, personal freedoms were diminished, letters were regularly opened and inspected, public gatherings were prohibited, and all residents were issued passes that had to be produced whenever they left their homes and were approached by vigilant military and police authorities. Unauthorized searches became commonplace. Between 29 July and 2 October, when the Russian Army arrived in Galicia, Austrian authorities began shutting down Russophile and Pan-Slavic institutions, including clubs and newspapers. Surveillance was stepped up against Russophiles and Russian citizens. Some Russophile leaders, sensing the new threats to their movements, fled in time to Russia; others were arrested, such as Dmitrii Markov, who was charged with high treason on the day of the announcement of the mobilization.

Markov was one of dozens of Russophile activists who were charged with high treason in two trials during this period. The leaders of the Russian National Council (*Russkii narodnyi sovet*) were accused of creating a Carpathian Liberation Committee (*Karpatorusskii osvoboditel'nyi komitet*) for the separation of Galicia and Bukovyna, as well as Ukrainian-inhabited regions of northern Hungary. Ukrainophile witnesses gave hostile testimony during the trials, while the Poles stood by anxiously, hoping to turn Ruthenians against each other and thereby bolster their own authority. The Russophiles were further accused of recruiting volunteers to serve in the Russian Army, particularly among the membership of the *russkie druzhiny*, the armed bands of amateurs that had their counterparts on the Ukrainophile side in the Sich Sharpshooters. Eyewitnesses painted a picture of a wide-ranging conspiracy of priests, Russian-language teachers, and politicians who were eagerly awaiting the arrival of the Russian Army to achieve their liberationist or irredentist aims. The trial dragged on through 1915 and a second one began hearing evidence in Vienna in 1916. The trials became the subject of international negotiations when nearly all the accused were handed death sentences. Nicholas II appealed to Franz Josef through the Spanish King Alfons XIII, and the death sentences were commuted to life imprisonment.

In the meantime, however, the hostility that the trials provoked against Russophiles had the unfortunate consequence of spilling over to all Ruthenians, who became suspect even when they had clean records of loyalty to the dynasty. This hostility was especially common among military units serving in eastern Galicia and Bukovyna, and especially among those who did not know Slavic languages. Because the local words for Ruthenian—*rusyny, rusy, rusniaky*, and other similar ones—could sound to an untutored ear like Russian, many thousands of innocent Ruthenians, especially peasants, were caught up in the waves of arrests of Russophiles. The fate of those mistakenly arrested was to be sent to internment and concentration camps. As the treason hysteria spread in the first few weeks of the war, anyone with a vaguely Slavic-sounding name, even Poles, could be arbitrarily searched and arrested. And, given the Polish political elites' earlier support for the Russophile orientation in Galicia, they were not entirely innocent in the eyes of the authorities either.

The military units that transferred the prisoners to their internment camps and other sites of confinement often abused their charges with torture and arbitrary executions. Such behavior was documented and collected in one of the first publications about German (in this case Austrian, actually Hungarian) atrocities against the Russophiles and Slavic population more generally, the Talerhof almanacs.[1] Talerhof was the main camp designated for political prisoners; eventually, 30,000 people endured the ironically named *Thalerhof Freilager* (free camp). Before long these once-provisional sites were filled to overflowing with prisoners deemed to have a broad range of guilt; the authorities were overwhelmed, and conditions deteriorated quickly. Hunger and disease were widespread by the winter of 1915, but there was little that even conscientious camp wardens could do because the economic situation in the Habsburg lands quickly turned miserable. And despite a widespread awareness that many of those confined at various sites had no formal charges against them, the military bureaucracy worked painfully slowly to restore these unfortunates to some measure of greater liberty. Because of the perception of the internees as "conscious" enemies of Austria-Hungary, the prevailing conditions in the camps were far worse than those in prisoner-of-war camps. In addition to food shortages and the spread of diseases such as cholera and typhus, internees were particularly vulnerable to being exploited by local Austrian citizens who were supposed to guarantee provisions and services to the interned populations.

Of particular concern to the authorities were the Orthodox priests who were arrested in the early weeks of the war. As with the mistaken identification of those who called themselves *rusyny*, so too hundreds of Greek-Catholic priests were also indiscriminately arrested together with their Orthodox counterparts because the Byzantine ritual appeared to the ignorant or unsympathetic eye not significantly different from the Orthodox services themselves. And, once again, despite repeated appeals to Austrian authorities from both Catholic and Orthodox hierarchs and the creation of an investigatory commission in November 1914 to review all the cases of detained priests, little headway was made during the war. (Finally, in May 1917 the new Emperor Karl issued an amnesty to all remaining internees to return to their homes, and the camps were disbanded.)

Despite all these assaults on the Ruthenian population in Austrian lands, the evolution of the Ukrainian movement during the Great War nonetheless corresponded largely to the general pattern of Central and East European national politics. The Union for the Liberation of Ukraine and the Sich Riflemen, or Sharpshooters, both date their origins to 1914, as Joseph Pilsudski in Poland and Tamas Masaryk and Karel Kramar in the Czech case also viewed the outbreak of war as the beginning of their respective national liberations. Indeed, the successes of Pilsudski inspired young Ukrainian militarists, particularly in Galicia; Ukrainian sharpshooter societies were partly modeled on Pilsudski's *Strzelcy*.[2] The Central Powers viewed the "liberation armies" as potential cores for a German-Austrian–led occupation regime as well. The Germans early on experimented with such proto- and paramilitary formations for proto-states; the German-Polish Count Bogdan Hutten-Czapski, for example, attached to the German General Staff as resident expert on Polish and Ukrainian affairs, was commissioned to raise a German Polish Legion, the counterpart to Austria's sponsorship of Pilsudski's in Galicia, to incite resurrection in Russian Poland.[3] In Trebizond, Turkey, a German captain was commissioned to form a Georgian Legion for eventual support of the "liberation" of the Caucasus from Russian rule; and even a Finnish legion of volunteers was raised early in the war, though it only saw action in the spring of 1918. All of these efforts ultimately failed to meet the ambitious expectations of their sponsors, though many of them did play important roles after the collapses of the multinational dynastic empires.[4]

In important senses, the Austrians' decision to allow the formation of a Ukrainian volunteer sharpshooters' force was a logical outcome of Austria's historic policy of building a multinational army with national units,[5] though the Ukrainian legion was to be made up entirely of volunteers otherwise not eligible to serve in the imperial-royal army.[6] What was potentially incendiary about this move, however, was its timing in the heightened state of tension between the Russian Empire and Austria-Hungary as well as the particularly sensitive and complicated set of issues that were known as the "Ukrainian question." Moreover, the permission to outfit and recruit the new military formations involved the collaboration of exiles from the Russian Empire in ULU, who had already declared their determination to liberate Ukraine through the destruction of the Russian Empire. This was, therefore, a novelty in Austrian practice, and one that would have an important, if often tragic, role in the creation of the modern Ukrainian state.[7] The Austrians also very quickly learned to value the consequences of these experiments for their capacity to control a situation that was often out of their hands.

In early August Consul Emanuel Urbas served as the intermediary between the Ukrainian leadership in Galicia and the Army High Command (AOK), on creating a "volunteer Ukrainian legion" on the model of the Polish legion and as part of the Austrian National Guard (*Landswehr*). Kost' Levyts'kyi, on behalf of the Ukrainian National Council, called for a rifle corps of between one and five thousand men, to be trained and commanded preferably by Ukrainians, but "in no case Poles," and to be prepared for "the march against Kiev." Urbas optimistically estimated that 5000 men would be enlisted within ten to fourteen days. He described the banner that was under consideration for the new formations, one that combined the Ukrainian colors (blue-yellow) with the Austrian double eagle on one side and the Ukrainian lion and Austrian colors (black-yellow) on the other. Urbas promptly obtained assurances from AOK that the new legions would be outfitted and that wherever possible staff officers of Ukrainian nationality—and absolutely not Poles—would be assigned to the new troops. By early September, as the Russian Army was rapidly approaching Lemberg, the first 2,000 Ukrainian legionnaires took the oath of loyalty to the Emperor and Austria-Hungary and were attached to regular imperial and royal troops for security assignments. The taking of the oath to Austria-Hungary proved to be a temporary stumbling block in the growing cooperation between the Central Powers and the Ukrainians. Many of the legionnaires at first refused to take the oath and to serve on the front; instead, they insisted that they serve only in the rear areas of eastern Galicia and Bukovyna to protect Ukrainian lands from, among others, Pilsudski's Polish Legions.[8] The first commander of the Ukrainian legion, Michael Haluszczynskyi, a Lemberg gymnasium teacher, was typical of the first volunteers; nearly all of them were students and teachers.

Between the outbreak of war and the occupation of Galicia in September 1914, Austrian authorities came face to face with the new challenges that militarization of the empires' nationalities problems posed for future governance. Their analysis of those challenges also shaped the related discussions of changes that would be necessary after the anticipated Austrian reconquest of Galicia and the establishment of possible occupation regimes in Russian Ukraine after an anticipated (and much desired) Austrian victory over Russian troops. Austrian authorities were not unanimous in the conclusions they drew from these discussions and relied on often widely diverging evidence in support of their differences of opinion. Polish-Ukrainian antagonisms occupied the place of first importance in these policy discussions, but almost as important were the various evaluations of the loyalty of the majority of the Ruthenian population and the degree to which the Ukrainophile parties represented majority opinion in Galicia and Bukovyna.

The first dilemma, the historic rivalry between the dominant Poles and the still underrepresented Ukrainians, was posed in a stark form after the first roundup by Austrian authorities after the outbreak of war in Galicia. The putative targets of such arrests were hostile elements, among others, Russophile leaders and agents. Metropolitan Sheptits'kyi aroused the Ukrainian parliamentary delegation in Vienna to intervene on behalf of several prominent Ukrainian politicians, including deputies to the *Reichsrat*, who had been arrested, according to the Metropolitan, on false evidence given by malicious Polish lower-level bureaucrats. Following on these protests, the Army High Command issued a decree warning military authorities not to mistake those Ukrainians loyal to the Austrian Emperor (*kaisertreu*) for the enemy Russophiles, and not to rely on subjective evidence from Polish officials. (Unfortunately for all those concerned, Polish officials dominated at all levels of the Galician administration.) The High Command stressed the importance of this approach not only to secure the loyalties of Austria's Ukrainians, but to win the loyalties of Russia's Ukrainians by good example.[9]

The second dilemma, the political loyalties of the majority of Ruthenians, was posed in equally stark form after the first reports of Russophile collaboration with the invading Russian Army arrived from various intelligence sources. The Foreign Ministry's representative to the Army High Command reported to Vienna that such behavior had shaken many Austrian officials' convictions that Ruthenians were in their majority loyal to Austria and that the Russophile orientation embraced only a minority of Austria's subjects. One of the conclusions drawn from these initial reports was that the Ukrainian party leaders in Vienna and Galicia were largely without mass following—at least for now—and that any planned or ongoing collaboration with these leaders needed critical scrutiny. Not surprisingly, the Polish viceroy in Galicia, Witold Korytowski, similarly disputed any influence that Ukrainian leaders claimed over the population and warned that the masses remained susceptible to Russophile propaganda and pro-Russian sympathies. Korytowski even obliquely suggested that Metropolitan Sheptits'kyi himself, "whose loyalty to the [Austrian] empire was beyond doubt," nonetheless "lacked the necessary energy and insight into people that would keep him free from Russophile elements." Such skeptics also pointed out the so-far disappointing experience with the "Ruthenian Legion," as the Sich Sharpshooters were known. Not only were their numbers small, but their eagerness to enter battle seemed in question.[10]

Those who had more positive evaluations of the Ukrainian movement, notably Consul Urbas in the Foreign Ministry, reminded their colleagues that Poles had in the recent past supported the Russophile movement in Galicia—as a lesser threat than the Ukrainian parties—and had entered into tacit and more open collaboration with them even before the outbreak of war. Urbas even suggested that the Ukrainian movement showed far greater promise in aiding the Dual Monarchy in its current war than the Polish nationalists.[11] From all of this followed a recommendation to Vienna from Archduke Friedrich, Commander in Chief, that when Austria reoccupied these lands after the war it would be prudent to appoint a governor for a unified Galicia and Bukovyna who would treat the two primary populations, Poles and Ukrainians, more equally, and who would most likely, therefore, be from another nationality.[12]

Urbas also discussed possible occupation plans with Ukrainian leaders in Lemberg, among them Metropolitan Sheptits'kyi, who drafted a memorandum "on the organization of Ukraine with regard to military, social-legal, and church aspects and with the aim of its separation from Russia." This remarkable document, outlining the occupation regime for a victorious Austrian army, proposed the creation of an autonomous Ukraine under the Austrian Emperor. The foundation for the new Ukraine would be an autonomous Ukrainian army based on historic Cossack traditions; accordingly, the Austrian emperor would appoint a hetman who in turn would be assisted by a historian for issuing his universals to the army and people. Sheptits'kyi also recommended supplanting Russian legal norms with their Austrian counterparts and creating a unified Ukrainian church free from the control of the Holy Synod in Petersburg. Importantly, he suggested that these latter reforms in the religious sphere be introduced not by a government official, and especially not a military ruler, but by a clergyman. Perhaps not surprisingly, the Metropolitan of Galicia recommended his own offices for this task, given the Greek Catholic Church's traditional role as intermediary between Russian Orthodoxy and Roman Catholicism. Sheptits'kyi was not so naive as to believe that all bishops in Austrian-occupied Ukraine would agree to these measures, and warned that those who resisted ought to be replaced with men more sympathetic to Ukraine and Austria. What seemed so natural for a Greek-Catholic bishop accustomed to the institutions of national self-rule in Austrian Galicia, however, could only arouse the greatest alarm among Russian officialdom.

Consul Urbas, after his intensive discussions in Lemberg, reported that any hopes for a national uprising of Ukrainians in Russian Ukraine would depend on the success of the Austrian armies. He warned that Austria needed great goals for this war if it were to justify the tremendous bloodletting and suffering that would surely follow; the breaking of Russia's power and the creation of a free Ukraine "as far as the Don" were such worthy aims. Urbas also outlined a preliminary Ukraine policy for Austria after the defeat of the Russian Army and a set of propaganda appeals to the civilian population in the occupied territories. The most important, he insisted, was a redistribution of the land to the peasants (something his superior ruled out of the question), and also guarantees for the "language and faith of their fathers." The native Ukrainian population was to be involved as much as possible in the creation of schools, agricultural associations, and other institutions; prisoners-of-war might be reassigned to the Ukrainian volunteer corps or sent as agents into those regions not yet occupied by Austrian forces. He even identified those parts of the Russian Empire that had the most vital Ukrainian consciousness (Poltava, Chernigov, and Ekaterinoslav) and suggested what appeals might be made to Ukrainians in Russia.[13] The Austrian discussions were preempted for nine months by the occupation of Galicia by the Russian Army.

In conclusion, however, just as the policies of the Russian Army would prove unwittingly to reinforce mutually exclusive national identities in the territories in their temporary occupation, so too the policies of the Austrian and Hungarian authorities, abetted by their Polish collaborators in many instances, exacerbated the polarization of the Ruthenian population into pro-Russian and pro-Austrian enemy camps. And the measures, both those against the Russophiles and those intended to deepen the patriotic feelings of the Ukrainophile and Austrophile Ruthenians, were part of a broader geopolitical project of weakening the Russian Empire by detaching its western borderlands from the Russian heartland, thereby removing a major threat to the security of the Central Powers. Ukrainians found themselves unwittingly caught up in these geopolitical visions and many hundreds of thousands of innocent subjects on both sides of the border would suffer as pawns of the visionaries' ambitions. Still others, however, collaborated actively with or against one side or the other.

NOTES

1. *Talergofskii Al'manakh. Propamiatnaia kniga avstriiskikh zhestokostei, izuverstv i nasilii nad karpato-russkim narodom vo vremia vsemirnoi voiny 1914–1917 gg.* (L'vov, Izdanie "Talergofskogo komiteta," 1924–1934); part 1 – 1924; part 2 – 1925; part 3 – 1930; part 4 – 1932; annexes – 1934; Peter S. Hardy, ed., *Voennye prestupleniia Gabsburgskoi Monarkhii 1914–1917 gg. Galitskaia Golgofa, Kniga 1* (Trumbull, CT: Hardy Lane, 1964).
2. Roman Szporluk, *The Political Thought of Thomas G. Masaryk* (Boulder, CO.: East European Monographs; New York: Distributed by Columbia University Press, 1981), pp. 101–146; and Roman Szporluk, review of T. Hunczak, ed., *The Ukraine, 1917–1921, in Annals of the Ukrainian Academy of Arts and Sciences in the United States* 14 (1978–80), p. 268.
3. See Bogdan Graf von Hutten-Czapski, *60 Jahre Politik und Gesellschaft*, 2 Bde. (Berlin: E. S. Mittler, 1936).

4. Fritz Fischer, *Germany's Aims in the First World War* (New York: Norton, 1967), pp. 114, 134–135, 140. Characteristic of their preference for princely states, the Germans' favorite Georgian émigré in Berlin was one Prince Machabelli, who also advanced plans for a neutral Caucasian Federation.

5. On the multiethnic politics of the Austro-Hungarian armed forces, see G. E. Rothenberg, *The Army of Francis Joseph* (West Lafayette, IN: Purdue University Press, 1976); and Istvan Deak, *Beyond Nationalism: A Social and Political History of the Habsburg Officer Corps, 1848–1918* (New York: Oxford University Press, 1990).

6. The Sharpshooters traced their origins, to several earlier influences, including a sharpshooting movement in prewar L'viv, the influence of Polish sharpshooting circles, and secret student organizations in Galician high schools. In February 1914 the first courses were organized in the Austrian Army and a military fund was established by Galician Ukrainians to purchase weapons. In May 1914 the first NCOs passed their exams. See "History of ULU: Materials and Notes," National Archives of Canada (Ottawa, Canada), The Andry Zhuk Collection (hereafter Zhuk collection), MG 30, C 167, vol. 13, files 46–54. On the dealings of ULU with the Austrian and German governments on the creation of an armed force, see Theophil Hornykiewicz, *Ereignisse in der Ukraine 1914–1922 deren Bedeutung und historische Hintergruende*, 4 vols., (Philadelphia: Ferdinand Berger Printing House, 1966), vol. I, pp. 129–143; and Jerry Hans Hoffman, "The Ukrainian Adventure of the Central Powers," (Ph.d. dissertation, University of Pittsburgh, 1967), pp. 35–42.

7. On the political activities, see Kost' Levyts'kyi, *Istoriia politychnoi dumky halyts'kykh ukraintsiv 1848–1914*, 2 vols. (L'viv: p. a., 1926), pp. 720–722; on the Sich Sharpshooters, see Stepan Ripets'kyi, *Ukrains'ke Sichove strilets'tvo. Vyzvol'na ideia i zbroinyi chyn* (New York: Vyd. "Chervona Kalyna," 1956), pp. 17–76. Soldiers enlisted in the Sharpshooters during a mobilization in L'viv conducted by an organization called *Ukrains'ka boevaia uprava* (Ukrainian Combat Board).

8. See Hornykiewicz, *Ereignisse*, I, pp. 130–134; Hoffman, "The Ukrainian Adventure," p. 38.

9. Hornykiewicz, *Ereignisse*, I, pp. 16–17, 20.

10. Hornykiewicz, ibid, I, pp. 18–22.

11. Hornykiewicz, ibid., I, pp. 2–7.

12. Hornykiewicz, ibid., I, pp. 22–24.

13. Urbas was in Lemberg 2–15 August; for Urbas's correspondence with his superior, the Foreign Minister's chief of cabinet, Count Alexander Hoyos, and Sheptits'kyi's memorandum ("Pro memoria ueber die Organisierung der Ukraine in militaerischer, sozial-rechtlicher und kirchlicher Hinsicht mit dem Ziel ihrer Losloesung von Russland"), see Theophil Hornykiewicz, *Ereignisse*, vol. I, pp. 4–16. Hoyos rejected several of his agent's suggestions. And, curiously, Urbas himself felt a future Ukraine under Austrian protectorate status was not the ideal outcome of the war; he preferred a German protectorate owing to his expectation that Austria would be left responsible for Poland after the war.

CHAPTER 2
Russian War Aims and Wartime Propaganda

Exactly the same thing applies to Galicia. It is obviously disadvantageous to us to annex, in the interests of national sentimentalism, a territory that has lost every vital connection with our fatherland. For, together with a negligible handful of Galicians, Russian in spirit, how many Poles, Jews, and Ukrainized Uniates we would receive! The so-called Ukrainian, or Mazeppist, movement is not a menace to us at present, but we should not enable it to expand by increasing the number of turbulent Ukrainian elements, for in this movement there undoubtedly lies the seed of an extremely dangerous Little Russian separatism which, under favorable conditions, may assume quite unexpected proportions.
– Petr Durnovo, February 1914 [1]

THE GREAT WAR BEGAN OFFICIALLY with Austria's declaration of war against Serbia on 28 July 1914, followed by Germany's declaration against Russia four days later (and against France on 3 August). Austria's armies invaded Russian Poland on 19 August; Russia quickly mobilized two armies against East Prussia, while two Russian armies (III and VIII) invaded eastern Galicia on 18–19 August. Russian armies were defeated in the battles of Tannenberg and the Masurian Lakes by mid-September, but they were triumphant against Austria-Hungary in the battle of Galicia (18 August–21 September). The troops of Russia's Southwest Front, under the command of General Nikolai Ivanov, advanced 280–300 km into Austria-Hungary and occupied eastern Galicia and part of Austrian Poland. General Nikolai Ruzskii's III army captured Lemberg, the Galician capital, on 3 September.[2] General Ruzskii and VIII army commander General Aleksei Brusilov shaped initial policies for the occupation regime that was to evolve in Galicia; the history of that regime illustrates well the formulation and evolution of wartime policy. Army Chief of Staff Nikolai Ianushkevich also played an important role in shaping that policy.[3] In addition, the Foreign Ministry assigned its expert on Galicia, V. Olferev, to General Nikolai Ivanov's staff.

Despite Petr Durnovo's warnings about the risks involved in an occupation of Galicia, hotter heads prevailed in the imperial military leadership. From the start, Russian military propaganda supplied a version of Pan-Slavist faith that all Slavic peoples would welcome the liberating Russian Army and join the struggle against the Austro-Hungarian, and eventually Turkish, oppressors; accompanying this liberationist rhetoric was a related but somewhat contradictory message of irredenta, annexation, and unification, particularly with regard to Galicia and Bukovyna. After all, Russia had entered the war in defense of Slavic, Orthodox Serbia—and, by extension, for the liberation of all Slavs from their non-Slavic oppressors.

Emperor Nicholas II, in the imperial manifesto proclaiming the outbreak of war, set the tone for the propaganda campaign, "Following her historical traditions, Russia, united in faith and blood with the Slav nations, has never regarded their fate with indifference. The unanimous fraternal sentiments of the Russian people for the Slavs have been aroused to special intensity in the past few days, when Austria-Hungary presented to Serbia demands which she foresaw would be unacceptable to a Sovereign State."[4] The official organ of the Southwest Front, *Armeiskii vestnik*, published the liberationist proclamation of Grand Duke Nikolai Nikolaevich, Supreme Commander-in-Chief, to the peoples of Austria-Hungary:

> [I]n the name of the great Russian tsar I declare to you, that Russia, which has more than once shed her blood for the emancipation of peoples from foreign yokes, seeks nothing but the restoration of right and justice. To you, peoples of Austria-Hungary, she will now bring freedom and the realization of your national aspirations. . . . Russia . . . strives only that each of you might be able to develop and prosper, all the while preserving that precious legacy of your fathers—your language and faith.

He went on to say that "the Russian Army proclaimed itself as the liberator of oppressed peoples" and invited the Galician people to greet the "first clear day of free and peaceful labor."[5]

The appeal to the Galician people in the Grand Duke's proclamation hinted at the irredentist aspects of the war's quickly emerging aims. The commander of the invading Southwest Front's Eighth Army, General Aleksei Brusilov, expressed the irredentist agenda in his first orders to the troops on crossing the imperial borders: "We are entering Galicia, which, despite its being a constituent part of Austria-Hungary, is a Russian land from time immemorial, populated, after all, by Russian people (*russkim zhe narodom*)."[6]

Liberationist hyperbole of this kind became characteristic for all the major belligerent powers against their enemies,[7] but these rhetorical flourishes carried a grave risk of encouraging the disgruntled peoples of one's own multinational empire as well. Indeed, the war had the undesired consequence for the imperial elites of "internationalizing" their nationalities problems, according to which foreign powers claimed the authority to rearrange the ethnographic maps of their enemies' territory and to intervene on behalf of one or another national group, usually in the name of "liberation."[8] The Entente waged its war, among its other proclaimed aims, in the name of self-determination of nations. Of course, Britain, France, and Russia in particular had in mind the disintegration of the Habsburg and Ottoman empires, but the Russian nationality problem also became a sensitive area in Allied relations.[9] The Germans and Austrians, for their part, were much more active in promoting uprisings among the subject peoples of their major rivals—imperial Russia and the British Empire—and sponsored the conferences and publishing activities of several anti-imperial national groupings, including the Poles, Ukrainians, Lithuanians, Finns, Caucasians, Irish, Indians, and the Muslims. They also waged propaganda campaigns, at first rather primitive, to appeal to potential anti-Russian feelings among the non-Russians, including, ironically, a call to Germany's Zionist and non-Zionist Jews to rally their co-religionists in Russia against their rulers.[10] Despite the ostensible loyalty of the Germans to the monarchical principle, leading German military and political figures were ready to contemplate the overthrow of the Romanov dynasty in Russia.[11] The militant Pan-German movement appealed for a unification of the German Reich with all eastern lands occupied by German colonists. During the course of the war this movement gained in influence among those at the top of the German General Staff, especially in the coterie around General Erich Ludendorff. Although the Germans were the most consistent and enthusiastic backers of the anti-imperial national liberation movements, the Austrians were also closely involved with many such groups, particularly the Poles and Ukrainians.

The Russian Empire countered these moves with occasional rhetorical gestures that were meant to appeal to certain non-Russian national groups who might thereby be persuaded to support the Russian cause. The most notable and controversial was Grand Duke Nikolai Nikolaevich's announcement on 14 August 1914 that the Russian state might recognize an autonomous, reunited Poland within the Russian Empire after the war;[12] in fact, the Government made no firm commitments nor did it ease restrictions on Polish subjects during the war. However, in these and similar pronouncements the Russian government was beginning to articulate its war aims more clearly; among Russia's highest priorities was its determination not only to weaken the power of Germany and thereby future threats to itself, but also to take advantage of the opportunity to revise the borders of Austria-Hungary in Russia's favor. The apparent concessions to the Polish nation were central to both of those aims, and Foreign Minister Sergei Sazonov advised the tsar with the postwar settlement in mind. In November 1916 the Germans stepped up the propaganda war by announcing their intention of uniting Polish lands after the war in an independent Polish state. Whatever their motives, however, the belligerent powers inadvertently gave hope to more than just the Poles that their national dreams would be realized at the end of the war.[13]

The Pan-Slavic motifs of national liberation and irredentism were frequently accompanied by expressions of national unity that claimed the war was a cause that transcended all prior differences in the Russian Empire. Chairman of the State Duma Mikhail Rodzianko formulated the naive faith in an imaginary conversation with the enemy, "'Look at us,' we might say to them. 'You thought we were divided by strife and hatred, and yet all the nationalities dwelling in boundless Russia were welded into a single fraternal family when danger threatened our common fatherland.'" From the left, Alexander Kerenskii echoed these sentiments, which took on the status of a powerful myth with the imperial elites: "We believe that on the fields of battle, in great sufferings, the brotherhood of all the nationalities of Russia will be consolidated, and that there will be born a single will to free the country from its terrible internal shackles." Even a spokesman for the Jewish people, Deputy Friedman, joined in this patriotic rhetoric: "In this grand enthusiasm which has aroused all the tribes and nationalities of great Russia, the Jews march on the battlefield, shoulder to shoulder with all the other nationalities."[14]

Indeed, all of the nationalities who had representatives in the Duma made similar proclamations of national unity, but those proclamations masked the suspicions of loyalty that quickly rose to the surface once the war was seriously under way. For the Ukrainian national movement, the war between Russia and the Central Powers brought new trials and opportunities. By the eve of the war, Ukrainians of the Russian Empire had no official parliamentary representation in the State Duma; as such, they were denied the opportunity to pledge loyalty to the war effort as other nationalities had done. Leading Ukrainian intellectual and political figures, however, did join the voices of patriotic support for the war effort and promised social peace for the duration of the war. Nonetheless, because of Russian officialdom's suspicions that the Ukrainian movement was infiltrated by agents of the enemies, a new series of bans was imposed on Ukrainian cultural, educational, and political life. The only institutions that were not affected severely by the bans were the agricultural cooperatives. And many Ukrainian political leaders, harassed and persecuted by Russian authorities, had been in exile in Galicia since before the war.

The Russian Occupation Regime in Galicia[15]

Shortly after the outbreak of war, the Russian commander-in-chief, Grand Duke Nikolai Nikolaevich, issued two important proclamations, one to the oppressed peoples of Austria-Hungary more generally and a second to Poles in particular; both promised Russia's help in their "liberation" and restoration of historical justice. These liberationist appeals offered little by way of guidance to the invading Russian Army, however. Not surprisingly, the first Russian officials to set down guidelines for the occupation regime were the military commanders of the invading forces. General Brusilov's first orders allowed for local Austrian laws to continue operating and to be enforced by Austrian officials, unless they proved to be disloyal; those officials were to be monitored by "energetic staff officers," who were to proclaim that "the religious and civil freedom, as well as the lives, honor and property of peaceful inhabitants would be guaranteed and protected fully, if the local population refrained from all hostile activities."[16] This was in accord with new agreements on the law of war that had been worked out in the international meetings in the Hague and with the active support of the Russian tsar. The other guiding principle of the opening months of the war quickly came into conflict with the liberationist appeals, namely, the irredentist program of "reuniting" the "Russian people from the Carpathians to Kamchatka." That "reunification," in fact an annexation and unification for the first time in history under Russian tsars, was part of a consensus shared by imperial bureaucrats in the foreign, defense, and interior ministries, but also with liberal and conservative nationalists in the Duma and the press. The contradictions and political and institutional conflicts built into these contradictory war aims became one of many sources of division in wartime Russia.

Directly after the invasion, Kiev Governor-General Fedor Trepov had brief jurisdiction over the region and appointed several of his officials to Galicia.[17] The occupation regime was supposed to operate according to a 16 July (1914) law on military zones that decreed the supremacy of military commanders over all civilian authorities and opened considerable space for arbitrary actions by low-ranking officers in large regions of the country. In fact, the military regulations allowed for the emergence of the first form of dual power in the Empire; the laws that governed the rest of the Empire were suspended in the zones of occupation.[18] Still, both chief of staff Ianushkevich and Foreign Minister Sazonov requested the Council of Ministers to outline the general guidelines for the occupation regime, not only for the benefit of the occupation authorities themselves but also with the eventual postwar peace settlement in mind. Ianushkevich asked for clarification on several particular issues, all of which would prove vexing for the occupation authorities in the months ahead. They included demarcating the borders of a future Poland; deciding which empire's laws would be enforced; determining the general orientation on religious questions, especially the Uniate Church and conversion to Orthodoxy; and finally, the use of the Ukrainian language in occupied Galicia. (Ianushkevich opposed the use of the Ukrainian language and advised that it was prudent to tolerate some unofficial coercion in the matter of converting Uniates to Orthodoxy.) Sazonov wanted to preempt any allied attempts to decide the Polish question in particular by assuring that Russian rule and institutions were firmly in place in those areas under Russian control. The Council of Ministers' inability or unwillingness to come to any significant policy conclusions, however, left the field open for autonomous decisions and policy making--not only by military authorities but also by the various "experts" from the Duma and political parties, such as Nationalists Vladimir Bobrinskii and Dmitrii Chikhachev.[19]

The emerging dual authority in the Empire and the political conflicts built into the incomplete regulations for the occupation regime meant that the occupation forces had difficulty in establishing a firm and systematic policy. The first governor appointed to Galicia was Colonel Sergei Sheremet'ev, who turned, curiously, to pro-Russian Poles and, not surprisingly, pursued a Polonophile policy. Supreme Commander Grand Duke Nikolai Nikolaevich's proclamation on Poland was posted everywhere; Polish schools were reopened in Russian-occupied L'vov. But the local Russophile party grew alarmed with these tendencies and soon defeated Sheremet'ev's policies as too conciliatory with the Polish cause; they successfully agitated for his removal.[20]

Count Georgii Bobrinskii, a large landowner and sugar magnate,[21] was appointed as the second military governor-general of the newly conquered provinces; Bobrinskii governed the occupied provinces for nine months until a new Austro-German offensive sent the Russian armies into retreat. In line with Russian officialdom's long-term aims of integrating the new territories into the Russian imperial administrative framework, the *guberniia* model of provincial administration was extended to them; in the fall of 1914 L'vov, Tarnopol, Chernovets (and later Peremyshl) were all designated as *gubernii*.[22] Overall, the Galician administration answered to headquarters of the Southwest Front in Kiev, which was quickly becoming the de facto wartime capital of newly united Ukrainian lands. (For example, all cases of official malfeasance in the Galician governor-general's administration were to be tried in Kiev at the military district court there.) One of Bobrinskii's first assignments after his appointment was to develop more concrete and comprehensive guidelines for the occupation regime. Predictably, Bobrinskii's guidelines gave almost unlimited authority to military officials. (Foreign Minister Sazonov, meanwhile, proposed a stricter demarcation of civilian and military spheres of authority and recommended the appointment of a special commissar for civilian administration in Galicia. Sazonov shared the general consensus about the urgency of integrating the population and territory of the occupied areas into the legal and administrative frameworks of the Russian Empire.) An extensive report compiled by Bobrinskii's staff after the fall of L'vov to the enemy in June 1915 outlines the occupation regime's priorities and some of the ideas that guided their actions.[23]

The intentions behind Brusilov's initial orders in keeping Austrian officials in place enforcing largely Austrian laws were undermined by the flight of many of those officials with the retreating Austrian armies.[24] Two spheres of administration posed immediate challenges to Russia's adhering to international legal norms: courts and schools. Austrian courts did continue to function, though they were ordered to apply Austrian law "in the name of the Russian emperor" (and not the Austrian one), while Austrian officials' salaries were paid out of the Russian treasury. Before long, however, Russian officials began to complain about the contradictions that arose in applying foreign judicial norms in "their" new lands, as well as about the loyalty of the Austrian officials. Ianushkevich objected to several features of this liberal regime of allowing Austrian officials to proceed as if virtually nothing had changed. Firstly, he noted the prominence of Jewish, German, Hungarian, and other nationalities among the administrative officials of the judicial system; most of these groups he presumed to harbor hostile attitudes toward Russia. Secondly, Austrian officials conducted business in all the officially recognized local languages of the Austrian empire, including Polish, German, and Ukrainian (which departed from practice in the Russian Empire). Thirdly, Ianushkevich believed there to be too many judicial officials by Russian standards; this was an expensive luxury that could not be sustained. Ianushkevich came out strongly against maintaining Austrian courts and the use of non-Russian languages in those courts. Although Justice Minister Ivan Shcheglovitov rejected most of Ianushkevich's proposals as in violation of international law, in fact the military authorities got their way, for the most part. Shcheglovitov did agree to replace Austrian officials wherever possible with persons "devoted to the idea of the unification of local Slavs under Russian rule," and that the Russian language be introduced throughout the business of the courts. Not surprisingly the decision to introduce the Russian language in the courts created great confusion for the Polish judges, lawyers, and others who dominated those institutions.[25]

The second arena in which Russian military officials faced challenges to their mission of maintaining public order in the rear of the army was public education and, more specifically, the language of instruction in public schools. Russian activists and their local allies in the Galician Kachkovskii Societies identified schools and teachers early on as major instruments for the planned Russification of the population. Dmitrii Chikhachev set the broad outlines for education policy in his memorandum, written in his capacity as a deputy of the State Duma to Governor-General Bobrinskii. Chikhachev warned of the danger to Russia of schools in Galicia and Bukovyna, where teaching was conducted in Polish, German, and "the artificially created Ukrainian dialect." He proposed the closing of universities and other institutions of higher learning for an indefinite period, the immediate opening of Russian-language courses for teachers in eastern Galicia and Bukovyna, requiring the teaching of the Russian language in all educational institutions, and introducing all teaching staff and students to the Russian literary language, Russian history, geography, and literature. Chikhachev did allow temporarily for primary instruction in primary and secondary education to be conducted in local languages, including "the Little Russian dialect," but insisted on those languages' replacement by Russian as quickly as possible.[26] The influence of the Russophiles can be seen in the political-cultural occupation of Galicia that was marked by the symbolic triumph of the Russian language as the "expression of the Russian spirit." This new linguistic order was presented as the "restoration" of the Russian language, previously debased by the perfidious Austrian authorities. Panegyrics to the Russian language, the language of Pushkin and Turgenev, of Lomonosov and Derzhavin, were typically accompanied by expressions of contempt for the "new-baked language that passed as Ukrainian or Ruthenian," a creation of the Austrian occupation regime.[27]

Governor-General Bobrinskii's orders on education followed Chikhachev's recommendations fairly faithfully.[28] In mid-September all schools were temporarily shut down, then reopened on the condition that Russian-language instruction be introduced. Special Russian-language courses for teachers in eastern Galicia and Bukovyna were organized with official encouragement. Both the Ministry of Public Enlightenment and the Petrograd City Duma pledged themselves to subsidize Russian-language courses for Galician teachers. An energetic and enterprising founder of several educational institutions in Petrograd, Maria Alexandrovna Lokhvitskaia-Skalon, arrived in L'vov to organize courses in Russian language, literature, and history.[29] Much of this activity was coordinated by the Galician-Russian Benevolent Society, with its branches in Petrograd, Moscow, Kiev, Odessa, and other cities. The local affiliates raised funds for "our Russophile comrades" in Galicia and stipends for students who were willing to attend Russian-language universities and institutes.[30]

As a consequence of the flight of so many Austrian bureaucrats, but also because of the decision to introduce the Russian language in courts and schools, Bobrinskii saw no alternative but to appoint new officials from two important sources. First, in a departure from the more exclusively Polish orientation of his predecessor, he immediately turned to the Galician Russophiles for help; in addition, he had in his immediate entourage several officials known for their Russophile sympathies.[31] For all that, however, the occupation regime was staffed overwhelmingly by bureaucrats transferred from Kiev, Podolia, Volynia, and Warsaw. As is characteristic of such large-scale reassignments to occupation regimes, Russian bureaucrats took advantage of the opportunity to rid themselves of troublemakers or those with the least seniority, education, and experience. The consequences were understaffing at all levels and poor quality of administrative personnel.

Local administration was staffed with zemstvo activists, marshals of the nobility, zemstvo land captains, and officers transferred from army ranks. Local notables were admitted to administrative service if they demonstrated the requisite loyalty; moreover, the Russian nationalist and conservative parties, especially the Nationalist Party, the Octobrists, and Union of Russian People, were stronger in the southwest region than they were nearly anywhere else. They brought with them to Galicia their politics of neo-Slavic Great Russian imperialism, anti-Semitism, and hostility to Poles and Ukrainians.[32] Though the views of these new officials were likely to be closer to those of Vladimir Bobrinskii, Archbishop Evlogii, and the Nationalist and rightist parties, even those liberals, such as Pavel Miliukov, who criticized the right-wing for its extremism, attacked them not so much for the substance of their mission as for employing the wrong means.[33] Petr Struve, on the other hand, saw the initial Russian successes in Galicia as evidence of the superiority of the "Russian" way of organizing a multiethnic state over the Habsburg *Nationalitaetenstaat* and insisted that the Russian national principle be at the center of imperial policy.[34]

Spymania, Censorship, and the Policing of Political Loyalty: Ethnic Profiling as Policy

Spymania had already put down firm roots in the immediate prewar years and was hardly limited to the Russian Empire. Even before the war started the Council of Ministers had proposed a law on state treason that would deny foreigners suspected of spying of their right to trial; however, the Duma failed to pass the law before the outbreak of hostilities.[35] Before the occupation regime in Galicia was fully operational, the primary concern of the martial-law authorities was to prevent spies from carrying out their work in the region or from infiltrating from outside. Accordingly, they had broad authority over censorship, detention of suspected spies and other politically unreliable persons, and general movement in and out of the military zones. They immediately began introducing a security regime that was intended to control the movement of people, goods, and ideas in their zone and that involved a system of passes, with regulations for their issuance.[36] This frequently arbitrary rule almost immediately provoked conflict between provincial zemstvos, the Red Cross, and other civilian organizations, especially the Union of Towns and Zemstvos, conflicts that generally intensified over the course of the war; moreover, many military authorities refused to take punitive action against soldiers involved in pogroms against Jews, Germans, and other civilians in the front zones. For many liberal critics of the autocracy, Army Chief of Staff Ianushkevich personified the wartime authorities' obsession with spies and internal enemies, especially among Jews and Germans.[37]

All foreign citizens and "politically unreliable" persons were to be deported to the interior provinces of the Empire,[38] while an extensive system of surveillance was erected to keep track of large groups of less unreliable persons. The most obvious targets were clearly Germans and those who might be perceived as harboring sympathies toward the German and Austrian cause. Above all, the attention of the authorities was drawn to German subjects of Germany and Austria-Hungary resident in Russia, but very quickly Russian-subject Germans also became suspected of dangerous sympathies. The theme of German influence and conspiracies (*nemetskoe zasil'e*, also German dominance) everywhere became a commonplace in popular politics.[39] The front-line newspaper carried a regular rubric devoted to German machinations *and* German atrocities on the front, linking the two in highly explosive fashion, while military censors developed a category to keep track of all anti-German sentiments that might also undermine loyalty for the imperial family.[40] German-language publications were ordered closed. All correspondence, gatherings, and public conversations in German were banned.[41]

In a wave of Germanophobic hysteria and in coordination with their British and French allies, the Russian government decreed the alienation and sale of certain properties of persons related to subjects of Austria-Hungary and Germany.[42] The Ministry of Internal Affairs resolved to liquidate German colonization in the Empire, which had been the target of earlier campaigns by the Nationalist Party in the Duma. During the 1915 retreat German colonists were deported from Volynia; in southern provinces other German colonists were expropriated and, fearing deportation too, sold all their property in a panic.[43] The anti-German mood extended to the persecution of Baptists during the first months of the war. The Holy Synod complained that Baptist sects were conducting "propaganda" among the troops and in the trenches. Since the Baptists were of German origins, they were to be removed from the military theater and prosecuted.[44] Most explosive for the Army, given the considerable number of prominent military men of Baltic and other German origins, was the linking of the German question with the Baltic question.[45] Military men with German surnames began to worry seriously about their future at a time when even liberal Russians appeared to be infected with the jingoistic (*kvasnoi*) patriotism that the war had made acceptable. The alarm that this provoked is well illustrated by an episode recounted by Fedor Rerberg, an officer in the X Army Corps of the III Army during the initial campaigns of the war in Galicia and Poland, when a delegation of Russian liberals from the Khar'kov and Moscow Unions of Towns and Zemstvos arrived at the front with gifts for the victorious soldiers. Rerberg was repulsed by the demagogic manner of the civilian politicians, but felt especially uneasy with their virulent anti-German remarks. His superior officer warned him that the future could be full of risk for someone like himself with a German surname. This prompted Rerberg to defend the contribution that German-surnamed (and Finnish) officers had made in the Imperial Army; his outburst, however, failed to alleviate the anxieties he felt about the changed atmosphere.[46]

While the authorities mistrusted the Germans above all, the largest group of "political unreliables" was the Jews, who were equated with foreign subjects in many of the evacuation instructions.[47] The Galician Jews, who had enjoyed legal equality under the Habsburg monarchy, especially were viewed with considerable suspicion by Russian nationalist circles, who waged an energetic anti-Semitic campaign from the very beginning of the occupation. Many Galician Jews had indeed chosen to flee the occupied zone; their property was confiscated and designated for "poor peasants," who can be translated here as Ukrainian peasants. The martial-law regime press and Russian benevolent societies that descended upon Galicia to organize relief aid generally incited poor Ukrainian peasants against wealthier Jewish landowners.[48] Virtually all Galician Jews were viewed as potential spies or traitors, and a particularly vicious censorship, arrest, and deportation policy was implemented. Ianushkevich proposed the taking of Jewish hostages to discourage spies and traitors among the Jewish population. His proposal translated into orders from General Ivanov for hostage taking and deportation of prominent local residents.[49] (Most of these hostages and deportees were sent to Kiev, Chernigov, and Poltava provinces.)[50]

In the early months of the war, Jews had been particularly visible among the agents who were supplying the army in Galicia. On the pretext of the threat of widespread espionage on the part of these merchants and suppliers,

30

in February 1915 the Commander of the Southwest Front decreed a ban on the entry of any further Jews into the zone, as well as a ban on their movement from one province within Galicia to another.[51] Furthermore, because the military censor's office had no specialists in Yiddish, a ban on all publications and correspondence was implemented.[52] By the winter of the first campaign, this anti-Semitic wave extended to Jews who were Russian subjects and serving in various civilian support agencies, such as the zemstvos and the Red Cross. General Mikhail Alekseev eventually ordered that Jewish officials be removed from zemstvo organizations on the grounds that they were either avoiding military service or disseminating party propaganda.[53] Ianushkevich and Ivanov also began to raise the sensitive question of Jews serving in the army itself and advocated their exclusion. In any event, officers were ordered to follow closely the attitudes of Jewish soldiers toward the war and to monitor their performance during combat.[54] In this atmosphere of heightened suspicion toward Jews, the Southwest Command received numerous reports of units, especially forts, that without express authorization were either refusing to accept Jewish soldiers who were sent as replacements or transferring Jewish soldiers out of the region into the interior provinces.[55]

The attitudes and policies of the occupying regime toward other peoples of Galicia, primarily Slavic peoples, varied in their severity. Considerable attention was devoted to the preparation of special propaganda for Poles and other peoples of Austria-Hungary.[56] The Ministry of Foreign Affairs counseled their military counterparts to exercise a particularly humane policy toward the civilian population of Galicia, as well as toward prisoners-of-war, many of whom were Slavs. They even proposed, and this on 11 August 1914, that the military authorities consider the possibility of releasing prisoners who were Russians, Poles, Serbs, or other Slavs.[57]

Not surprisingly, the Poles presented a complicated picture. They were split into at least two camps, one still hoping for a change in Russian Imperial policy and indeed collaborating with the Russian occupation authorities,[58] the other casting its fate with the Central Powers. Russia's official position was now pro-Polish in imperial proclamations and appeals. Because the Austrian authorities had permitted Polish *Sokol* groups to function, Russian authorities sanctioned the existence of similar groups on Russian-occupied territory as well.[59] Still, after Galician Jews, it was the Poles who attracted the most attention from counterintelligence, who suspected every Pole of being a potential spy. Agents kept lists of Poles suspected of espionage and delivered regular reports on the Polish revolutionary movement.[60] And Russian authorities were well aware that the Austrian High Command had allowed Pilsudski to form Polish Legions on Austrian soil, among whose recruits were Polish exiles from Russia. Thousands of Galician Poles were deported out of the rear zones of the Southwest Front, especially priests who persisted in delivering sermons "in a separatist spirit" and members of illegal Polish political parties and organizations.[61]

For eastern Galicia, however, the overriding goal of the occupation regime was the unification of Galician Rus with the Russian Empire, and here the focus of attention was on the Galician Ukrainians, or, in the worldview of the Russian authorities, the Galician Russians. The Foreign Ministry, in its note to the War Ministry, recommended reopening the Russian-language newspaper, *Prikarpatskaia Rus' (Carpathian Rus)*, which had been closed down by Austrian authorities.[62] The Russian authorities hoped thereby to take advantage of the aura of popular resistance that the Russophile party had recently come to enjoy after many of them were arrested by the Austrians, detained in prison in Hungary, and even executed.[63] The Foreign Ministry expected that the majority of Uniates in Galicia actually were inclined to prefer the Orthodox Church, but would need to be handled with tact if their conversion were to be successfully achieved. At the same time, all social and cultural organizations were to be shut down until their political orientation could be ascertained, the local *sejm* ought not to be convened, and no concessions ought to be made to the Ukrainian separatist movement because of its intention to "undermine the unity of the Russian tribe" (*russkogo plemeni*); nor was any mention to be made of a separate Ukrainian language.[64]

These views were generally shared by Governor-General Georgii Bobrinskii, who saw his major task as the fusion of the region with the Empire in both "the political and national senses." In his inaugural speech in L'vov, he proclaimed his faith that eastern Galicia and the Lemko lands were "native (*korennye*) Russian lands and should be ruled according to Russian principles."[65] Bobrinskii subscribed to a view of the local Galician Slavs as members of the Little Russian branch of the Russian people who had been artificially torn from the Russian state and Orthodox Church by the pernicious policies of the Habsburg authorities and their Polish henchmen. He also shared the widespread belief that the Ukrainian movement for autonomy and for the unification of all Little Russians existed thanks only to the support of Austria-Hungary. Accordingly, Bobrinskii recognized the pro-Russian National Rada as the genuine spokesmen for the Galician Slavs. (The Rada had changed its name at the beginning of the war to the Russian People's Organization, whose organ was the Popular Council.) The Rada, according to Bobrinskii, had suffered up to 40,000 arrests at the hands of the Austrians for its Russophile politics. The rural population expected an end to the persecutions and domination by Galician Poles and Jews.[66] Shortly after the invasion of Galicia, General Brusilov entrusted Vladimir Bobrinskii with the task of freeing all those political prisoners in Austrian jails who had suffered for their Russophile politics. Brusilov recalled that Bobrinskii took up this mission with particular dedication since he had had close ties with the Russophile party among the Ruthenians before the war.[67]

Following from these views, the occupation authorities arrested and deported thousands of other Ukrainian political, religious, and cultural leaders,[68] and banned the posting and distribution of all materials in Russian or Little Russian *narechii* that had been published beyond the frontiers of the Russian Empire, as well as materials printed in other languages, "if the content of these books was hostile to the Russian government and Russian people." Furthermore, all Ukrainian bookstores had to be closed "because of the tendentious, anti-Russian character of the publications that were being sold."[69] In effect, the measures revived the restrictions on the Ukrainian language from the period before the 1905 revolution (the Ems *ukaz* and Valuev decree).

The first proclamations of the Supreme Command went out to "our liberated Russian brothers" and promised freedom to all Slavs who would accept Russian citizenship. This was found to have encouraged large-scale surrenders, but among those who surrendered, military intelligence uncovered many Ukrainian soldiers with "Austrophile" orientations or former revolutionaries (including Ukrainian Social-Revolutionaries and Social-Democrats) who were intent on spying for the enemy.[70] Any apprehended members of the battle groups of the Socialist Revolutionary party or "anarchist-communists" were to be arrested and exiled to the northern provinces of Russia.[71] As part of a series of legal and administrative measures taken by Russian officials that began to transform the understanding and meaning of citizenship in the Russian Empire, Bobrinskii ordered a change in the release procedure for arrestees, allowing only prisoners of the local Galician population who were either of "Russian origins" or Uniate or Orthodox faith and "whose loyalty to Russia could be attested to by Galician notables."[72] Predictably, Bobrinskii turned to the Russophile activists of the

Russkii *narodyni sovet* for help in determining the political reliability of the population; later the Interior Ministry also responded favorably to the Russophiles' offer to monitor political loyalty in the occupied territories.[73] Henceforth as well, military censors were ordered to keep special track of letters in which separatist views were advocated.[74] The Ukrainian movement in both Galicia and in Russia's southwest provinces came under renewed attacks during the war and was treated by intelligence officials as one large network of spies, terrorists, and traitors. Professor Myhailo Hrushevs'kyi was the most prominent Ukrainian activist arrested in Russia; he was linked to the activities of the Union for the Liberation of Ukraine, which was operating out of Vienna after its headquarters was evacuated from L'vov.[75]

Not only did such repressive measures provoke considerable resentment and protest among the local Ruthenian population, but before long even the formerly loyal Russophiles grew disenchanted with the occupation regime. "One might have expected," reported Governor-General Bobrinskii,

> that the Russo-Galician intelligentsia, who belonged to the party of the Russian People's Organization, might have been more favorably inclined toward our initiatives, but this intelligentsia expected too much for itself from Russian authorities and above all [they expected to be] summoned to the highest posts in the region; second-tier appointments did not satisfy them and among their midst formed a group who was dissatisfied and openly critical of the activities and decrees of the Russian authorities. The people of this party did not want to understand that it was impossible for a Russian government to appoint people so full of hate and hungry for revenge against the Poles and Jews for their many years of previous oppression.

Bobrinskii concluded that "these people" were ungrateful for the encouragement that the Russian authorities gave them in opening their cultural centers and press organs. Bobrinskii nonetheless wanted to avoid repressive measures, not the least because of the aura of being fighters for the Russian idea that this party enjoyed among the local population.[76]

Eventually Governor-General Bobrinskii's policies were criticized as too conciliationist and moderate, and he also earned the hatred of the Nationalists and the right-wing activists, who had descended upon Galicia from elsewhere in the Russian Empire. After their aspirations were blocked by Governor-General Bobrinskii, many of the prominent Russian nationalists turned to his cousin Vladimir and to Archbishop Evlogii and began a campaign of underground intrigues against the official occupation regime, and stepped up pressure for a more thoroughgoing Russification.[77] Besides the conflict between Bobrinskii and the Holy Synod's appointee, to be described below, the Governor-General also had tense relations with the military authorities, many of whom were also sympathetic to the increasingly radical Russification politics of Evlogii, the Governor-General's cousin Vladimir, and their local Russophile collaborators. An example of these conflicts was the fate of the front-line newspaper. In October 1914 *L'vovskoe voennoe slovo* became the official organ of the Commander of the Southwest Front, under the editorship of N. F. Narkevich. The newspaper enjoyed the unique privilege of operating without any censorship and Narkevich launched a series of attacks on the major individuals forcing the pace of Russification. They responded on the pages of the daily *Kiev*, which accused Narkevich in turn of Ukrainophilism. The Commander of the Southwest Front reprimanded Narkevich and *L'vovskoe voennoe slovo* was temporarily suspended and replaced by *L'vovskii vestnik*, the official organ of the military governor-general himself. The conflict between the Russophiles and Bobrinskii's administration reached its high point in January 1915. But shortly thereafter, in March, the military newspaper was revived, with Narkevich back as the editor.[78]

One other matter that emerged late in the occupation not only tested the Russian imperial elite's ideological views of Galicia, but also impinged on its war aims, namely, the possibility and means of conscription of local Galicians into the Russian Army. In the spring of 1915, shortly before the German and Austrian offensive, which forced the Russian evacuation eastward, the Russian Popular Council (*Russkii narodnyi sovet*) in L'vov, the local Russophile umbrella organization, petitioned the occupation authorities to grant permission for the formation of a "special Galician-Russian volunteer detachment," as well as permission for Galician-Russian students to enroll in Russian Imperial military schools. On 27 May, Lt. General Matornyi answered Count Georgii Bobrinskii, the Military Governor-General of Galicia, that the General Staff saw no reason not to proceed with the formation of such Galician-Russian *druzhiny* following the principles laid down for the Czech units; nor did the General Staff object to enrolling Galician-Russian students in Russian military schools, provided they were fluent in the Russian language. Bobrinskii was advised to ascertain the opinion of the Commander of the Southwest Front.

By this time, the Russophiles could point to the formation of numerous volunteer detachments among Slavs recruited in the Russian Empire. The Russians, motivated in part by the utopian Pan-Slavic ideals shared by a considerable part of their ruling elites, began experimenting with national military units practically simultaneously with their rival empires. This marked a very dramatic departure from traditional Russian military conscription and manpower policies, unlike those for the Austro-Hungarian armed forces where national units were the norm.[79] Arguing that "Slavic brethren nations" were groaning under Habsburg oppression and eagerly awaiting their moment to join the Russian cause of liberation,[80] as early as 6 August 1914, the General Staff was seriously discussing the formation of Czech, Slovak, and Polish units, but also considered decidedly non-Slavic Finnish and Latvian ones as well.[81] The Czech, Slovak, and Polish units were to be formed from among the large and rapidly growing population of Austro-Hungarian soldiers in Russian captivity, tens of thousands of whom were held in a camp at Darnitsa near Odessa. Émigré Czech societies volunteered to help form the units with the express aim of fighting against Austria-Hungary, fomenting uprisings there among their compatriots and "liberating their motherland from Austrian enslavement." The War Ministry won unanimous approval from the Council of Ministers on 30 August for the formation of two infantry regiments in the Kiev Military District. An All-Russian Guardian Society for Captive Slavs (*Vserossiiskoe popechitel'stvo o plennykh slavianakh*)[82] was founded to conduct charity and propaganda work among these groups—which eventually added Slovenes, Serbs, and Croatians to their concerns—and to acquaint Slavic POWs with Russia's liberation mission.[83] The War Ministry acknowledged that because these units were being authorized primarily out of political considerations, they needed to be treated differently in matters of staffing. The Czech volunteers, for example, were not likely to have much military training since they were largely political exiles. At first Russian officers would be assigned to the units with the eventual aim of creating a Czech officer corps as well.[84]

Despite the generally positive orientation of the High Command toward the experiments in national military formations,[85] the discussions about Galician *druzhiny* bore no fruit at the time because of the successful Austrian offensive of the late spring and summer. Later in the year, however, the Ministry of Foreign Affairs once again raised the issue of enrolling former Austrian Slavs who had accepted Russian citizenship into Russian military schools, acknowledging also the need for some sort of loyalty check and generally advising caution regarding those who had transferred their loyalties. Finally, two years later when Iulian Iavorsky raised the question of forming a volunteer Carpatho-Russian *druzhina* in the Russian Army, Matornyi asked for a copy of his letter to Bobrinskii.[86]

"I Will Deliver Sheptits'kyi--Dead or Alive": Confessional Politics: A Case Study in Occupation Policy and the Dilemmas of Russian Nationalism

It was religious policy perhaps more than anything else that turned many once-loyal Russophiles and potentially neutral Galician peasants against the Russian occupiers. Here the conflicts within the Imperial administration revealed a dangerous lack of unity of will both at the top of the edifice and between the top and the men who were directing wartime policy on the ground. More importantly, the irredentist myths and Russian nation-building project that united Russian officialdom and nationalist public opinion foundered on the reality of a powerful and deeply entrenched Greek-Catholic Church organization in Galicia. The intense rivalry between the Holy Synod in Petrograd, and more specifically the Synod's plenipotentiary to Galicia, Archbishop Evlogii (who arrived in L'vov on 6 December 1914), and Metropolitan Andrei Sheptits'kyi was at the center of a religious civil war in the occupied territories over the spiritual identity of Galician (and Bukovynan) Ruthenians. Both sides were inclined to cast the struggle in titanic terms, as between the rival axes of power, with Rome (Vatican)-Vienna-Lemberg pitted against Petrograd/Moscow and Orthodoxy.[87]

In a letter to the Pope dated 18 August 1914, Sheptits'kyi explained, "A war between our Emperor and the Tsar of Moscow is underway. They are fighting the war for us (*za nas*), because the Muscovite Tsar can not tolerate the fact that in the Austrian state we have freedom of religion and nationality." In remarkably similar terms but from a diametrically contrasting viewpoint was Archbishop Evlogii's address "To the Galician-Russian nation and clergy," in which he insisted that the political unification of Galicia be consolidated by a spiritual unification of the Greek Catholics with the Orthodox Church. He called for the clergy to follow their national conscience and return their flock to the "faith of your fathers, that faith, in which your sacred ancestors had lived and found salvation until the end of the seventeenth century." (This is a reference to the Union of Brest in 1596 and its aftermath.) Evlogii insisted, in accord with the irredentist myth of neo-Slavist Russian nationalists and imperialists, that even though Galician-Russians had been raised in the "traditions of the Latin Union, it could not have smothered your Russian spirit." In the Orthodox Church's utopian vision, Uniate pastors would lead their flock "along that path of organic union with great Russia and especially restore and strengthen their ancient historic union with the Orthodox Russian Church."[88] For the Orthodox hierarchy, the preservation of the Uniate Church implied sanctioning its legitimacy and raised the specter of its revival in the Russian Empire itself. This was seen as entirely anathema; hence the fervent hopes that prewar conversions of several borderland villages to Orthodoxy were the true way of the future.

Shortly after Russian troops crossed the border into eastern Galicia, the Holy Synod convened a special session to discuss the "organization of religious and moral life for the Russian population of Galicia." The outcome of those deliberations was the appointment by the tsar of Evlogii, Archbishop of Volynia and Zhitomir, to tend to the spiritual needs of the Orthodox population of Galicia. (As Archbishop of Volynia and Zhitomir, Evlogii by tradition served as exarch of the Patriarch in Constantinople for Galicia and Carpathian Rus.) Evlogii's appointment provoked anxieties in Polish Catholic and Ukrainian circles among those who remembered his role in the Kholm question, on which he and Vladimir Bobrinskii had allied in the Duma to combat the Polonizing influences of the Catholic Church. Evlogii and Archbishop Antonii of Khar'kov were considered the Church's leading Ukrainian experts and were dedicated to combating the Uniate Church and especially its clergy. Still, Evlogii's experience during the last prewar years had led him to conclude that the process of conversion to Orthodoxy would be long and difficult, despite the apparently loose religious loyalties of the borderland population generally, and could not be forced because of the authority enjoyed by the Greek-Catholic clergy.[89]

This opinion was confirmed by a special commission sent to Galicia in the fall of 1914 by the Ministry of Interior's Department of Spiritual Affairs, the agency responsible for non-Orthodox religious matters; moreover, one of the commission's members reported that while some of the Uniate bishops were ready to swear their loyalty to the Russian state, they were unanimous and categorical in their refusal to change religious identities. The official suggested that while the Uniate clergy might be relied upon to disseminate all-Russian ideas (*obshcherusskie idei*), they could not be similarly counted on to advocate Orthodoxy.[90] The determined opposition of the Uniate clergy forced Russian military, civilian, and religious authorities to consider alternative tactics in their mission to spread Orthodoxy. Evlogii advised the Synod to tolerate the parallel existence of two churches and support vigorous Orthodox missionary work in Galicia, in the expectation of the eventual triumph of Orthodoxy in this confessional rivalry. The Synod accepted Evlogii's recommendation and directed him to begin negotiations with the Uniate bishops on the conditions of coexistence of two churches in the occupied territories; the negotiations foundered on several irreconcilable issues.[91]

In this war of faiths proclaimed by Sheptits'kyi and Evologii, the martial-law authorities had a seemingly overriding mission: to keep the rear of the fighting army secure and the population at peace. But the circumstances in which they were operating did not bode well for that essential military mission. According to military Governor-General Bobrinskii, with the advance of Russian forces into Galicia many Roman and Greek Catholic priests, the latter primarily "Mazepists" in Bobrinskii's characterization, had fled their parishes and departed with the retreating Austrian armies. Once the local population was assured that the Russian forces were not hostile to them, they began, according to Bobrinskii, to return to their parishes and request the appointment of Orthodox priests. Bobrinskii saw his task at this time as the prevention of any re-Catholicization of the local population, which translated into surveillance of the remaining Catholic and Uniate clergy, and several arrests and deportations to interior Russia, the most notable being the arrest of the Greek-Catholic Metropolitan Andrei Sheptits'kyi, his confessor (a priest in the Basilian order that had been another target of imperial Orthodox campaigns), the rector of the L'viv Theological Seminary, and others in Sheptits'kyi's entourage.[92]

Sheptits'kyi had long been suspected of encouraging Ukrainian separatists and the union of the Orthodox Church with Rome, which, in Russian eyes, meant the conversion of Orthodox believers to Catholicism. The Police Department had evidence of Sheptits'kyi's efforts to establish the Uniate Church in Russia, including the recruitment of Russian Orthodox and Old Believer priests to the Basilian Order, the purchase of lands in the Russian Empire that bordered Galicia with the intention of resettling Russian Uniates from Galicia there, the persecution of Russian Orthodox priests in Galicia, and even the outfitting of a detachment of "Mazepist" sharpshooters. Russian intelligence authorities claimed that Sheptits'kyi had agreed to plans for religious expansion drawn up in the event of the occupation of Little Russia by Austria-Hungary, including establishing Greek-Catholic eparchies.[93] Ianushkevich promised to deliver Sheptits'kyi "dead or alive" to the Ministry of Interior and said he would not hesitate to kill him if the need arose.[94] General Brusilov summoned the Metropolitan to his headquarters and effectively placed him under house arrest after warning Sheptits'kyi that he would be held responsible for any hostile actions on the part of the local population. After a few days, the Metropolitan and his entourage were deported to Kiev.[95] The arrest provoked diplomatic protests abroad, not only from the Vatican but also in allied countries of western Europe and America; Aleksandr Kerenskii raised the issue in the State Duma and part of the Russian press censured the government for this act.[96]

Despite these arrests, Bobrinskii announced an official policy of religious tolerance—at least as far as Christians were concerned—and urged the local and arriving Orthodox clergy to exercise extreme caution in their dealings with the local population. In the absence of firm guidelines from the Holy Synod, Bobrinskii required that a 75 percent majority of the local population of a village or town be established by voting before an Orthodox priest would be sent, but he also insisted that no Uniate or Catholic priests be allowed to return from hiding to their parishes. Bobrinskii's policy was quickly criticized by the conservative Russian newspaper *Novoe vremia* as too liberal to defend the interests of Orthodoxy.[97] He also came under pressure from the activists of the Galician-Russian Society, which had worked out its own program on the religious question, one considerably more radical than the governor-general's or Evlogii's, at least according to his own account of the period. The ever-active Vladimir Bobrinskii, who criticized the governor-general for inappropriately intruding on the prerogatives of the Holy Synod, and Dmitrii Chikhachev proposed an immediate closing of the Basilian and Jesuit orders, the dismissal of Greek-Catholic bishops "who were attempting to Latinize the Eastern rite," a ban on all agitation against Orthodoxy, and, most seriously, the expulsion of Uniate priests from the villages. To replace the expelled Uniate priests, the Society advised sending in Orthodox priests "familiar with the Little Russian dialect and the mores and practices of Red-Rusians; they also advocated turning over Uniate churches to Orthodox priests after half of the parishioners indicated their willingness to convert. Bobrinskii claimed he had the approval of the army's chaplain, protopresviter Shavel'skii and the Grand Duke. Another commission from the Interior Ministry descended upon Galicia in November and gave further encouragement to the radical policies of the Galician-Russian Society.[98]

Well before Evlogii finally arrived in L'vov on 6 December, local Russian authorities and their allies from the Galician-Russian Society had provoked religious civil war in dozens of villages by expelling Uniate priests and replacing them with Orthodox clergy who began streaming into Galicia. In these increasingly tense conditions, the governor-general tried unsuccessfully to delay the arrival of the Archbishop, fearing his presence would only exacerbate matters. Instead, on Vladimir Bobrinskii's suggestion, Evlogii promptly served a mass in the city's main Uniate cathedral and delivered a sermon that was interpreted as a death sentence on the Uniate Church. With every passing month of the occupation, Uniate priests were perceived as the enemy and the base of Ukrainian nationalism, and they organized resistance to Russification of the region. The gap between the governor-general's official policy and local practice grew wider and wider as local authorities interpreted the policy to mean that if Uniate priests refused conversion they were to be expelled from their parishes. They thus began to order dismissals, transfers, and appointments of Orthodox clergy from the interior provinces of the Empire to Galicia, often in violation of the 75 percent majority policy. Governor-general Bobrinskii, now joined by Army Chaplain Shavel'skii, blamed Evlogii's incendiary presence for the trouble and charged that his appointments were substandard, the quality of Orthodox priests being much lower than the Uniates they were replacing, and that the Orthodox clergy were isolated and suffering materially because they had been removed from their native parishes. Evlogii persuaded Nicholas II to approve the unprecedented financing of salaries for Orthodox priests in Galicia. In any event, Evlogii made no effort whatsoever to coordinate his behavior with the hierarchy of the military chaplaincy. Such arbitrary actions, according to Bobrinskii, had even more alarming consequences during the evacuation, when tens of thousands of Galicians were compelled to flee with the departing Russian forces out of fear that they would be persecuted by the reoccupying Austrian forces or by local fellow parishioners.[99]

The primary result of these arbitrary actions was widespread discontent with Russian authorities in the occupied territory.[100] Despite the entreaties of both Bobrinskii and Brusilov to the Synod and the General Staff, Evlogii was allowed to pursue his independent policy and to threaten the peace of the martial-law regime that local military and civilian authorities tried so hard to preserve until the tsar's visit to L'vov in April 1915. Even though

General Brusilov had resisted Nicholas's visit as premature, Evlogii's enemies were able to win the tsar over to their argument that the Archbishop was a threat to the stability of the rear. To the great relief of the governor-general, the tsar recalled Evlogii back to Volynia and resolved to entrust the matter of the Uniate faithful in Galicia to another person.[101] Evlogii wrote a secret report to Oberprokurator Sabler in which he recommended "the establishment of an Orthodox L'vov eparchy; the seizure from the Greek Catholics of St. George's Cathedral, the metropolitan's palace, and the Dormition and Transfiguration churches in L'vov with all their possessions; and the closure of all Basilian monasteries and confiscation of their property by the state."[102]

1. Durnovo's opposition to the annexation of Galicia was part of his general warning to the tsar in early 1914 to avoid war with Germany because of his fears that such a war would end in violent social—and likely socialist—revolutions in both Russia and Germany. Durnovo served briefly as Interior Minister (1906–07) and later in the State Council, where he belonged to the group of rightist members (*gruppa pravykh*). See F. A. Golder, ed., *Documents of Russian History, 1914–1917* (New York: The Century Company, 1927), p. 12; the full text of Durnovo's memorandum appears at pp. 3–23.

2. For more on these initial battles, see Norman Stone, *The Eastern Front 1914–1917* (New York: Charles Scribner's Sons, 1975), chapters 3–4; A. Beloi, *Galitsiiskaia bitva* (Moscow/Leningrad: Gosizdat, 1929); and N. N. Golovin, *Iz istorii kampanii 1914 goda na russkom fronte. Galitsiiskaia bitva: pervyi period do 1 sentiabria novago stilia* (Paris: Rodnik, 1930); and *Iz istorii kampanii 1914 goda. Dni pereloma Galitsiiskoi bitvy (1–3 sentiabria novago stilia)* (Paris: Rodnik, 1940). Golovin surveys the southwestern theater in appendix 1 of his 1930 volume; that theater covered the Galician province of Austria-Hungary and the Kiev and Warsaw Military Districts.

3. Ianushkevich was reputed to have been one of the most pathological anti-Semites among Russia's leaders. See W. Bruce Lincoln, *Passage Through Armageddon: The Russians in War and Revolution* (New York: Simon & Schuster, 1986), pp. 141–142; and Alfred Knox, *With the Russian Army, 1914–1917*, 2 vols. (New York: Dutton, 1921) vol. I, p. 290. As Chief of Staff, Ianushkevich was among the most vocal military officials who regularly denounced Germans, Jews, and Ukrainians as spies and agents of the Central Powers. See Michael Cherniavsky, *Prologue to Revolution: Notes of A. N. Iakhontov on the Secret Meetings of the Council of Ministers, 1915* (Upper Saddle River, NJ: Prentice-Hall, 1967), pp. 39–40, 56–57.

4. Imperial Manifesto, 2 August 1914, in Golder, *Documents*, pp. 29–30.

5. Ibid., 16 September 1914, p.1. The Army was also portrayed as the liberator of Carpathians in Ugorskaia Rus' and of Romanians from the Turkish yoke.

6. Brusilov's order is cited in M. K. Lemke, *250 dnei v tsarskoi Stavke* (Minsk: Kharvest, 2003), p. 199.

7. Study of wartime propaganda began not long after the war itself. See Harold D. Lasswell, *Propaganda Technique in World War I* (New York: P. Smith, 1927); Hans Thimme, *Weltkrieg ohne Waffen* (Stuttgart and Berlin: Cotta, 1932); Antoni Szuber, *Walka o przewage duchowa. Kampanja propagandowa koalicji 1914–1918* (Warsaw, 1933). In a recent study of propaganda in Austria-Hungary, Mark Cornwall reminds us that nearly all the attention in these early histories has been on the Western Front or the Allied propaganda effort. See his *The Undermining of Austria-Hungary: The Battle for Hearts and Minds* (London: Macmillan Press, 2000), p. xii.

8. Marc Ferro, "La politique des nationalités du gouvernement provisoire (fevrier–octobre, 1917)," *Cahiers du monde russe et sovietique* 2 (1961), p. 136.

9. The British, for example, pushed for liberalizing the status of Jews in the Russian Empire. See Cherniavsky, *Prologue to Revolution*, pp. 56, 71–72.

10. Ferro, "La politique," pp. 133–134; for an example of German appeals to the Empire's Muslims, see Knox, *With the Russian Army*, I, pp. 232–233. The Committee for the Liberation of the Jews of Russia was to be the German vehicle for winning adherents among Russia's Jews, but the Zionist organizations quickly declared a policy of neutrality between the belligerent powers. See Seppo Zetterberg, *Die Liga der Fremdvoelker Russlands 1916–1918. Ein beitrag zu Deutschlands antirussischen propagandakrieg unter den fremdvoelkern Russlands im ersten Weltkrieg* (Helsinki: Finnish Historical Society, 1978). Very early in the war, General Helmuth von Moltke, chief of the General Staff, outlined to the Foreign Office his plans for inciting national revolutions in Poland, Finland, and the Caucasus. The classic study of Germany's plans for national revolutions remains Fritz Fischer's *Germany's Aims*; see especially pp. 84, 98–106 for Bethmann Hollweg's September program; for the Germans' plans for eastern Europe, see pp. 113–117, chapters 4 and 5.

11. The German Ambassador in Copenhagen, Count Ulrich von Brockdorff-Rantzau, openly advocated the overthrow of the Romanov dynasty and warned the German Emperor against continuing "to attach serious weight to our traditional relationships with Russia." Fischer, *Germany's Aims*, pp. 152–153.

12. "Proclamation of the Supreme Commander-in-Chief [Grand Duke Nicholas]," 14 August 1914, in Golder, *Documents*, pp. 37–38. Nicholas's proclamation already hinted at the possible undesired consequences of the resurrection of the Polish nation: "There is only one thing that Russia expects of you, --an equal regard for the rights of those nationalities with which your history has linked you."

13. During the initial campaigns on the Caucasian Front, the Caucasian Viceroy and Commander of the Caucasian Army Illarion I. Vorontsov-Dashkov, who was widely known as sympathetic to the cause of establishing an Armenian nation, provoked conflicts with his field commander, General Nikolai Iudenich, over the former's strategy of forcing a rapid offensive. Several Caucasian deputies to the Duma, notably Nikolai Semenovich Cherniavsky, also criticized Vorontsov-Dashkov for taking such politically motivated strategic risks. Iakhontov, *Prologue*, pp. 36–37.

14. Duma speeches, 8 August 1914, in Golder, *Documents*, pp. 33–37. These sentiments were likewise repeated in the resolution adopted unanimously by the State Duma, though the extreme left deputies left the hall to avoid voting against the resolution.

15. The best study of the occupation regime is a recent book by a Russian scholar who adds much new information from imperial archives: A. Iu. Bakhturina, *Politika Rossiiskoi Imperii v Vostochnoi Galitsii v gody Pervoi mirovoi voiny* (Moscow: AIRO-XX, 2000). For older accounts of the Russian occupation, see Feliks Przysiecki, *Rzady rosyjskie w Galicyi wschodniej* (Piotrkow: Wyd. "Wiadomosci Polskich," 1915); Josef Bialynia Cholodecki, *Lwow w czasie okupacji rosyjskiej (3 wrzesnia 1914–22 czerwca 1915)* (Lwow, 1930); Bohdan Janusz, *Dokumenty urzedowe okupacyi rosyjskiej* (Lwow, 1916), and his *293 dni rzadow rosyjskich we Lwowie* (Lwow, 1915) and *Odezwy i rozporzadzenia z czasow okupacyi rosyjskiej Lwowa, 1914–1915* (Lwow, 1916); Ivan Petrovych, *Halychyna pidchas rosiis'koi okupatsii: serpen' 1914-cherven' 1915* (L'viv: Politychna Biblioteknya, 1915); A. Cholovskii, *L'vov vo vremena russkago vladychestva* (Petrograd, 1915); and Marzell Chlamtacz, *Lembergs politische Physiognomie waehrend der russischen Invasion* (Vienna, 1916).
16. Cited in M. K. Lemke, *250 dnei v tsarskoi Stavke* (Minsk: Kharvest, 2003), p. 202
17. Trepov's jurisdiction as governor-general also included Podolia and Volynia gubernii; he had been serving as governor-general since his appointment in December 1908.
18. Those areas under the military's formal jurisdiction included the two capitals, Petrograd and Moscow, Transcaucasia, and the western borderlands, the latter inhabited by large non-Russian populations. See "Polozhenie o polevom upravlenii voisk v voennoe vremia," St. Petersburg, 1914, described in Daniel Graf, "Military Rule Behind the Russian Front, 1914–1917: The Political Ramifications," *Jahrbuecher fuer Geschichte Osteuropas*, Neue Folge, Band 22 (1974), Heft 3, pp. 390ff.
19. Bakhturina, *Politika*, pp. 60–69. The Council of Ministers devoted several meetings to discussion of these issues and resolved to demarcate the borders according to ethnographic statistics; in the end, western Galicia was to be treated as eventually entering into a reconfigured postwar Poland, whereas eastern Galicia was to be annexed to the Russian Empire more directly. For more on the Council of Ministers' deliberations during the war, see *Sovet ministrov Rossiiskoi Imperii v gody pervoi mirovoi voiny. Bumagi A. N. Iakhontova (Zapisi zasedanii i perepiska).* (St. Petersburg: Dmitrii Bulanin, 1999).
20. "Halychyna i Bukovyna pid rosiis'koiu okupatsiieiu," Zhuk collection, vol. 9, file 24.
21. Archbishop Evlogii speculates that Bobrinskii (1863–1928) was chosen to head the occupation regime because of the popularity of his cousin, Vladimir Alekseevich, leader of the Galician-Russian Benevolent Society and Duma deputy from the nationalist fraction. Bobrinskii's brother, Count Aleksei Aleksandrovich, was an appointed member of the State Council and leader of the right faction. See Evlogii, *Put' moei zhizni*, p. 253. Another prewar Nationalist Party ally of Vladimir Bobrinskii's who was influential in the Bobrinskii administration was Dmitrii N. Chikhachev, a specialist on the "Kholm question."
22. Mikhail Mel'nikov, governor of Volynia, was appointed governor of the new L'vov province; I. L. Chartorizhskii was appointed governor of Tarnopol. Colonel Aleksei Skallon, previously head of police in Kiev and Minsk, soon replaced Major-General Eikhe as mayor (*gradonachal'nik*) of L'vov.

23. "Otchet kantseliarii voennogo general-gubernatora Galitsii v period vremeni s 28/VIII. 1914 po 1/VII. 1915," RGVIA (Russian State Military-History Archive) f. 2003, op. 2, d. 539, ll. 1–85; and "Otchet vremennogo voennogo general-gubernatora Galitsii po upravleniiu kraem za vremia s 1-go/IX. 1914 g. po 1-go/VII. 1915 g.," ll. 1–26.

24. Because the police officials fled together with the retreating Austrian armies, the local municipal officials organized a volunteer force to preserve order in L'vov, in which citizens willing to collaborate with the new authorities served. Fedor Rerberg, "Istoricheskie tainy velikikh pobed i porazhenii, predatel'stva i revoliutsii. Desiatyi armeiskii korpus na poliakh srazhenii pervogo perioda Velikoi Voiny," unpubl. ms. (1925), Hoover Institution Archives, p. 48.

25. Bakhturina, *Politika*, pp. 85–89.

26. Chikhachev's memorandum, "Po uchebnomu delu v Vostochnoi Galitsii i Bukovine," is cited in Bakhturina, *Politika*, pp. 91–92. Chikhachev met with the curator of the Kiev school district, A. N. Derevetskii, to discuss collaborating on a new administrative structure for education in Galicia. Chikhachev's views were shared by Vladimir Bobrinskii, who also authored an influential memorandum "O iazyke v Galitsii i Bukovine."

27. The lead editorial of *Armeiskii vestnik* (18 September 1914) described a tumultuous "rehabilitation" of the Russian language: "The streets, public buildings and hotels of L'vov are covered in Russian signs; on the squares and street corners, the Russian newspaper *Prikarpatskaia Rus'*, recently closed by the Austrian government, is being sold; displayed in the windows of book stores is *The Grammar of the Russian Literary Language*, for which the author, Semën Iu. Bendasiuk, sat in an Austrian jail for two years. Poles, Jews, Germans, and Armenians, all are studying Russian." Bendasiuk and Iulian Iavorskii, émigrés from Galicia, arrived from Kiev with the occupying army to establish the Russian language in a prominent position.

28. Bobrinskii issued his circular to Galician governors, "O shkolakh i obshchestvakh," on 27 September 1914; see Bakhturina, *Politika*, pp. 91–93.

29. *Sovet ministrov Rossiiskoi Imperii v gody Pervoi mirovoi voiny*, pp. 117, 386; Tiander, *Das Erwachen Osteuropas*, p. 50; "Otchet," RGVIA f. 2003, op. 2, d. 539, l. 22. The Russian Ministry of Enlightenment opened only ten elementary schools during the occupation; the Synod, however, was far more active and opened nearly fifty schools during the same period.

30. Besides the *Galitsko-russkoe blagotvorite'noe obshchestvo*, several other ideologically allied organizations were active in occupied Galicia: *Slavianskoe blagotvoritel'noe obshchestvo, slavianskie komitety*, and several *tserkovnye bratstva*. At the head of all of them stood Vladimir Bobrinskii. "Halychyna i Bukovyna," Zhuk collection, vol. 9, file 24.

31. Included among these were Ostrogradskii; for special assignments, he appointed the Russophiles Volodymyr Dudykevych, M. Glushkevich and Semen Labenskii, editor of *Prikarpatskaia Rus'*.

32. Among the prominent Kiev organizations was the Carpatho-Russian Liberation Committee (*Karpato-Russkii osvoboditel'nyi komitet*), whose chairman was Iulian Iavorskii. For a list of Bobrinskii's closest staff appointments, see "Otchet kantseliarii," RGVIA f. 2003, op. 2, d. 539, ll. 1–85. Most of the appointees came either from the chancellery of the governors-general of Kiev, Podolia, and Volynia, or from the zemstvo staffs of those provinces. Bobrinskii's report concluded that Russian police officials were particularly ill-equipped by their education and experience to administer the new lands, and provoked the considerable resentment of the local population. On the prominence of Russian nationalist organizations in the southwest provinces, see Robert Edelman, *Gentry Politics on the Eve of the Russian Revolution: The Nationalist Party, 1907–1917* (New Brunswick, NJ: Rutgers University Press, 1980).

33. See Miliukov's views in *Rech'*; for a sample of the views in the Russian press, see Count Aleksei N. Tolstoi, "Pis'ma s puti," *Russkie vedomosti* (7 November 1914), in which he highlights the poverty of the Ruthenian villages; it seemed to him "that even the cows bowed down to us." Dmitrii Vergun, in a report from L'vov, complained of the historic violation of Russian rights in Galicia because of the policy of bilingual signs (Russian and Polish!), "Ustroenie Galitsii," *Novoe vremia* (28 November 1914). In an editorial in *Rech'* (2 November 1914), the author quipped that so many Russian politicians and Duma deputies had descended upon L'vov that if the Austrians were to suddenly recapture the city Russia would be left without its lower house. Among the prominent Kadets who arrived to help with Red Cross and Zemgor efforts were Igor Demidov, Lashkevich, and Vasilii Maklakov.

34. "Very likely, for many in the Russian intelligentsia before the war anational [*beznatsional'naia*] Austria represents their ideal of state organization . . . Many, perhaps only because of the fact of war in 1914 have understood that Russia is strong as a nation-state [*natsiona'noe gosudarstvo*] . . . Russia is not simply a nation-state . . . but precisely a nation-empire [*natsional'naia Imperiia*]. Russian nationality in this nation-empire is not only the dominant, but the cementing element." *Birzhevye vedomosti* (23 December 1914); quoted in A. Iu. Bakhturina, *Politika Rossiiskoi Imperii v Vostochnoi Galitsii v gody Pervoi mirovoi voiny*, p. 8.

35. Eric Lohr, *Nationalizing the Russian Empire: The Campaign against Enemy Aliens during World War I* (Cambridge, MA: Harvard University Press, 2003), p. 18.

36. "O vvedenii v Kievskoi gubernii voennoi tsenzury," RGVIA f. 1759, dop. op., d. 1406. For special instructions on the administration of territories of Austria-Hungary occupied by Russian troops, see *Vremennoe polozhenie ob upravlenii oblastiami Avstro-Vengrii, zaniatymi po pravu voiny*, RGVIA f.2003, op.2, d. 691, ll. 26–28. See also procedures for arresting spies and for deporting all Chinese merchants from the border region to the interior of Russia.

37. Iakhontov recorded the concerns about Ianushkevich among the members of the Council of Ministers; see Cherniavsky's *Prologue to Revolution*, pp. 39–40, 56–57, inter alia; for more comprehensive evidence of Ianushkevich's attitudes and actions, see Sergei Nelipovich, "General ot infanterii N. N. Ianushkevich: 'Nemetskuiu pakost' uvolit' i bez nezhnostei: deportatsii v Rossii 1914–1918 gg.," *Voenno-istoricheskii zhurnal* 1 (1997): 42–53.

38. RGVIA f. 1759, dop. op., d. 1410.

39. When rightist leader Aleksei Khvostov became Minister of Interior in September 1915, he declared that the war on German dominance was one of the three most important issues facing the nation. See Eric Lohr, *Nationalizing the Russian Empire*, pp. 68, 104.
40. *Armeiskii vestnik*; RGVIA f. 1759, op. 4, d. 1843, ll. 495–496. Among others, John Armstrong has even suggested that Nicholas II felt compelled to enunciate such a virulently anti-German line precisely "to divert attention from the notoriously German atmosphere of his Court." See his "Mobilized and Proletarian Diasporas," *The American Political Science Review* 70 (1976): 399.
41. On the German ban, see Fleischhauer, *Die Deutschen*; see also V. S. Diakin, "Pervaia mirovaia voina i meropriatiia po likvidatsii tak nazyvaemogo nemetskogo zasil'ia," *Pervaia mirovaia voina 1914–1918* (Moscow, 1968), pp. 227–238.
42. Robert W. Coonrod, "The Duma's Attitude toward War-time Problems of Minority Groups," *ASEER* 13 (1954): 30–38. Elsewhere in the Empire, anti-German riots shook Moscow in June 1915. Conservative and rightist deputies from the Duma called for the annihilation of the Baltic nobility. In particular, members of the German Naval Union were arrested or deported. On the confiscation of German property and discriminatory economic measures during the war, see Fleischhauer, *Die Deutschen*, pp. 479–522; and Eric Lohr, *Nationalizing the Russian Empire*, chapters 2–3.
43. See *Armeiskii vestnik* (16 October 1914), p. 4; and David Rempel, "The Expropriation of the German Colonists in South Russia during the Great War," *Journal of Modern History* vol. IV (1932): 49–67. During the summer of 1915, Headquarters presented Agriculture Minister Krivoshein with a proposal to award soldiers who distinguished themselves in battle with land endowments from, among other sources, the confiscated estates of German colonists and enemy subjects. The measure was not enacted. See Cherniavsky, *Prologue*, p. 22.
44. Letter dated 28 June 1915. RGVIA f. 1759, op. 3, d. 1420.
45. See *Armeiskii vestnik* (2 November 1914). The censors' reports were full of the following sentiment: "We are fighting against the Germans, but our leadership in Russia is all Germans. Who commands the Russian soldiers? Germans. You know very well that the Germans are winning everywhere without a fight." RGVIA f. 1759, op. 4, d. 1846, l. 88. This particular report is dated 1916. During the fall of that year the censor reported, "They do not cease writing about the German preponderance." f. 1759, op. 4, d. 1870, l. 255 ob.
46. See his "Istoricheskie tainy," Hoover Archives, esp. pp. 161–165. Rerberg devoted most of his preface to combating the prevalent notion that the war had been the consequence of German-Slavic rivalry.
47. See "O poriadke vyseleniia inostrannykh poddannykh i evreev vo vnutrennie gubernii Rossii i vyezde za granitsu inostrantsev," RGVIA f. 1759, dop. op., d. 1421.
48. In 1915 a notorious right-radical, the editor of *Zemshchina*, Ivan Rodionov, was appointed editor of the official newspaper of the South-West Army, *Armeiskii Vestnik*. Loewe, *Antisemitismus*, p. 147n.

49. For Ianushkevich's proposal, see RGVIA f. 2003, op. 2, d. 539, ll. 23–25; Ivanov's order to take hostages was dated 22 September 1914. On the deportations of the Jews, see "Iz 'chernoi knigi' russkago evreistva, materialy dlia istorii voiny, 1914–1915," *Evreiskaia Starina*, vol. X (1918), pp. 231–253; also "Dokumenty o presledovanii evreev," *Arkhiv russkoi revoliutsii*, I. V. Gessen, ed., vol. XIX (Moskva: "Terra," 1991), pp. 245–284. This did not prevent Russian officials from seeking out Jews to work as spies in the newly occupied territories of Galicia and Poland. See Rerberg, Hoover Institution Archives, "Istoricheskie tainy," pp. 14–15.
50. On hostages, see Bakhturina, *Politika*, pp. 193–194; the hostages included bank directors, city managers, local intelligentsia, and merchants. See also Eric Lohr, *Nationalizing the Russian Empire*, pp. 142–145, 148.
51. RGVIA f. 2003, op. 2, d. 539, l. 9.
52. "Prikaz No. 389," 19 September 1914. RGVIA f. 1759, op. 4, d. 1843, ll. 9, 219–22. The censors' files are full of confiscated letters in Yiddish.
53. Loewe, *Antisemitismus*, p. 149; RGVIA f. 2003, op. 2, d. 950. Ivanov complained that zemstvo institutions employed as many as 11 percent Jews and that their numbers in the Red Cross and All-Russian Union of Cities' employees was also too high. He demanded a cap of 5 percent for these organizations, and that no Jews at all be employed on sanitary trains. RGVIA f. 2003, op. 2, d. 701, ll. 12–17. From the archival evidence, military authorities spent much of their time compiling lists of Jews in various branches of the civilian and military administration.
54. RGVIA f. 2003, op. 2, dd. 701–702. The military authorities even devised a special questionnaire to ascertain the loyalty of Jewish soldiers. RGVIA f. 2067, dd. 3784, 3786; f. 2003, op. 2, d. 701, ll. 10–12. Ivanov wrote that "without fail at the end of the war we shall have to most seriously discuss the possibility of keeping Jews in the ranks of the army, or, in any case, the diminution of their numbers in combat units."
55. RGVIA f. 2003, op. 2, 701, l. 4. As of 20 March 1915, the Southwest Command reported 180,000 Jews in its units.
56. RGVIA f. 2067, op. 1, d. 3852.
57. On 31 July 1914, all Austrian and German male subjects between the ages of 18 and 45 were declared POWs and designated for deportation, except Rusyns, Czechs, and Serbs. RGVIA f. 1759, op. 3, d. 1420, l. 1. These measures were gradually refined to appeal to all potentially loyal Slavs among the Ottoman and Habsburg Empires. The archives reveal a fascinating conflict over the designation of who could be considered a foreign subject in wartime conditions and what sorts of differentiated policy could be developed to take advantage of the complicated sets of loyalties. See f. 1759, op. 3, d. 1420.
58. See Przysiecki, *Rzady rosyjskie*, and Cholodecki, *Lwow w czasie okupacji*.
59. RGVIA f. 2003, op. 2, d. 323, l. 106. Permission was granted on 24 August 1914.
60. RGVIA f. 2067, op. 6/c, dd. 70, 232. The proclamation of Polish statehood by Grand Prince Nikolai Nikolaevich in the first days of the war was not popular among many military circles; when Fedor Rerberg came upon a cache of anti-Russian materials of various Sokol and Polish Legion organizations after the Imperial Army crossed into "Russian" Poland, he condemned the Imperial policy with harsh sarcasm, "*These* are the people we gave autonomy and freedom!" He noted how sharply the hostile attitude of the ungrateful Poles toward the Russian Army contrasted with the generosity and good will of most Galicians during the recent entry of the Imperial Army there. "Istoricheskie tainy," pp. 82, 155.

61. "Vypiska iz spiska poliakov neblagonadezhnykh v politicheskom otnoshenii i vrazhdebnykh russkoi Gosudarsvtennosti, prebyvanie koikh v tylu armii Iugo-Zapadnogo fronta nezhelatel'no i vredno," RGVIA f. 1759, op. 3, d. 1410, l. 24.

62. The Council of Ministers decided to finance the newspaper, published by the *Russkii narodnyi sovet*, as a vehicle for disseminating "true and favorable" news about Russia and the Russian Army. Bakhturina, *Politika*, p. 96.

63. During the retreat of the Austrian Army, troops, especially Hungarian Honveds, unleashed a wave of terror on the local population. The internment camp in Styria, Talerhof, and the Austrians' repressive policies served as potent symbols for the Russian national and military press. See Peter S. Hardy, *Voennye prestupleniia Gabsburgskoi monarkhii 1914–1917 gg: Galitskaia golgofa* (Trumbull, CT: Hardy Lane, 1964).

64. RGVIA f. 2003, op. 2, 691, ll. 9–13. See the list of societies, museums, and credit associations to be suspended in "Halychyna i Bukovyna pid rosiis'koiu okupatsiieiu," Zhuk collection, vol. 9, file 24. This file also includes the 4 October decree forbidding the functioning of all such societies, with a fine of 3,000 rubles or three months in prison for all violators.

65. See Bobrinskii's speech to the notables of occupied L'vov on 10 September 1914. An important symbolic moment in Bobrinskii's campaign for integration was the inauguration of direct rail service between Kiev and L'vov. See *Armeiskii vestnik* (8 November 1914), p. 4, for the announcement and commentary on its significance. *Armeiskii vestnik* carried regular feature articles of Russian visitors to Galicia who would marvel at how similar were the natives to their Russian brethren. See, for example, "Iz galitskikh vpechatlenii," 27 November 1914, or a series of articles written under the pseudonym of El'-Es' (real name Leonid Zakharovich Solov'ev) about the "restoration" of the lands to Russia. The Emperor himself visited L'vov to reaffirm the "historic ties" of Galicia to Russia (9 April 1915). See also a reference work for military officers published by the Commander-in-Chief of the Southwestern Front in July 1914, *Sovremennaia Galichina. Etnograficheskoe i kul'turno-politicheskoe sostoainie eia, v sviazi s natsional'no-obshchestvennymi nastroeniami.*

66. "Otchet," RGVIA f. 2003, op. 2, d. 539, ll. 2–4. After the Russian organizations of Galicia sent a telegram to Emperor Nicholas II, the Emperor replied with his salutations to the "long-suffering Russian people." *Armeiskii vestnik* (18 September 1914), p. 3. The tsar was proclaimed as a unifier of Russian lands and the Russian Army as having cleansed Red Rus' from its centuries-long enslavers. The theme of Austrian repressions against Russophiles and spies was a regular feature in *Armeiskii vestnik*. (See 21 September 1914, p. 4.)

67. A. A. Brusilov, *Moi vospominaniia* (Moscow: Voenizdat, 1983), pp. 86–87. Bobrinskii, though a member of the State Duma, was also a former guard in the Life-Hussars, and had volunteered for military service after the outbreak of war.

68. Dmytro Doroshenko, *Moi spomyny pro nedavne-mynule 1914–1920* (Munich: Ukrainske Vid-vo, 1969), pp. 42–43.

69. "Otchet," RGVIA f. 2003, op. 2, d. 539, p. 21; p. 23. The bookstore of the Shevchenko Society was closed on 22 September 1914. Bobrinskii's instructions on censorship were published in the next day's issue of *Prikarpatskaia Rus'*.

70. Counterintelligence agents were ordered to be especially vigilant in uncovering former revolutionaries or pacifists who might have been drafted into the Austrian army and captured by the Russians. For example, a special search was conducted for one Vladimir Stepankovskii, who was known to have been hiding abroad since 1907 after he had stood trial for his membership in the Kiev Revolutionary Organization *Spilka*. He had fled to London after being released on bail. In 1914 he joined the Austrian army. Elsewhere, military authorities expressed concern about the Austrians' opening a school in Kaway to prepare spies with all sorts of assignments, primarily among Poles, but also among Jews and Rusyns. RGVIA f. 1759, op. 3, d. 1414, ll. 101–102, 219–220, 339–340, 355, 357.

71. Military intelligence kept close track of the Ukrainian SRs in particular. "Ustanovlenie nabliudeniia za litsami, prinadlezhavshimi k boevoi gruppe partii S-R i gruppe anarkhistov-kommunistov," RGVIA f. 1759, dop. op., dd. 1423, 1445, 1453. Military intelligence compiled lists of conscripts who had police records for special surveillance. A typical case was one Zhabotinskii and his associate Zelenyi, who belonged to the "party of Ukrainophiles." RGVIA f. 1759, op. 3, d. 1423, ll. 269–270; see also ll. 101–112, 320.

72. By the end of the first occupation regime, only 4,290 soldiers had been so released from captivity. "Otchet," RGVIA f. 2003, op. 2, d. 539, l. 9; on easier conditions for persons of Slavic origin to become Russian subjects, see "Ob oblegchenii uslovii perekhoda lits slavianskogo proiskhozhdeniia v russkoe poddanstvo," RGVIA f. 1759, dop. op., d. 1420.

73. Bakhturina, *Politika*, p. 194.

74. RGVIA f. 1759, op. 4, d. 1843, l. 364.

75. The Police Department of the Russian Interior Ministry summarized its surveillance and repressive measures against the Ukrainian movement (*ukrainstvo*) for the first two years of the war in a special memorandum, "Zapiska ob ukrainskom dvizhenii za 1914–1916 gody s kratkim ocherkom istorii etogo dvizheniia, kak separatisko-revoliutsionnago techeniia sredi naseleniia Malorossii," RGIA, Pechatnaia zapiska 410, no. 262. I thank Eric Lohr for sharing his copy of this remarkable document.

76. "Otchet," RGVIA f. 2003, op. 2, d. 539, ll. 4–5. Before Bobrinskii arrived in L'vov, the military authorities had closed all Polish newspapers, the Russophile *Prikarpatskaia Rus* and *Golos naroda* (Little Russian edition), as well as the Ukrainophile *Dilo*. All Jewish newspapers were likewise forbidden. During 1915 Bobrinskii permitted the opening of new Russian-language newspapers in L'vov, *Novyi krai* and *Chervonnaia Rus'*. Even after he sanctioned the reopening of *Prikarpatskaia Rus'*, however, the editor continually complained of overly restrictive censorship rules. That the Russophiles had great aspirations that were blocked under Bobrinskii is confirmed by ULU reports from occupied territory in "Halychyna i Bukovyna pid rosiis'koiu okupatsiieiu," Zhuk collection, vol. 9, file 24.

77. Evlogii, *Put' moei zhizni*, pp. 189–229.

78. "Otchet," RGVIA f. 2003, op. 2, d. 539, p. 23. Georgii Bobrinskii also confiscated *Prikarpatskaia Rus'* and one of the more fanatical sermons of Archbishop Evlogii; moreover, Bobrinskii forbade the prominent local Russophile Dudykevich from appearing at the audience with the Governor-General on New Year's Eve. It was the Austrian offensive that forced both sides to finally reconcile. "Halychyna i Bukovyna pid rosiis'koiu okupatsiieiu," Zhuk collection, vol. 9, file 24; Ivan Petrovych, *Halychyna pid chas rossis'koi okupatsii* (L'viv, 1915), pp. 83–95.

79. On this, see Mark von Hagen, "The Limits of Reform: The Multiethnic Imperial Army Confronts Nationalism, 1874–1917," in *Reforming the Tsar's Army: Military Innovation in Imperial Russia from Peter the Great to the Revolution*, ed. David Schimmelpenninck van der Oye and Bruce Menning (Cambridge, UK: Cambridge University Press, 2004).

80. "The victory of General Ruzskoi's army has just removed the obstacle which has prevented the Russian spirit and language from broadly flourishing in the provincial life of Galicia. From the very annexation of it [Galicia] to Austria, Russian Galicians [*russkie galichane*] have been struggling for the Russian faith, the Russian name, the Russian language." *Armeiskii vestnik*, 18 September 1914, p. 1.

81. RGVIA f. 2003, op. 2, d. 323. On the formation of Polish *druzhiny*, see also f. 2000, d. 3882; f. 2003, op. 2, d. 691, l. 35. The first request, from Kholm province, to form Polish volunteer detachments for the Russian Army is dated 20 August 1914. *Armeiskii vestnik* (9 October 1914) announced that Polish Legions had been formed on the Russian side with the permission of the Supreme Commander-in-Chief.

82. RGVIA f. 2003, op. 2, d. 544, ll. 78, 80–81, 101–102, 129. The Ministry of Internal Affairs approved the Society's charter.

83. RGVIA, f. 1759, op. 3, dd. 461, 477.

84. RGVIA f. 2003, op. 2, d. 323, ll. 16, 161. In the discussions about the Czech units, the War Ministry invoked an earlier precedent during the Russo-Japanese War when a Colonel Madritov formed a regiment of Chinese volunteers to fight against the Japanese. The first Czech unit, incidentally, was formed in Kiev by 12 September 1914. For more on the formation of the Czechoslovak *druzhina*, see V. S. Dragomiretskii, *Chekhoslovaki v Rossii 1914–1920* (Paris/Prague, 1928), pp. 10–28; and John F. N. Bradley, *The Czechoslovak Legion in Russia, 1914–1920* (New York: Columbia University Press, 1991), pp. 5–24.

85. Very quickly the Russian High Command came to view the Slavic POWs as a reliable source of reinforcements and a trustworthy labor force. In May 1915 General Alekseev, as Commander-in-Chief of the Northwest Front, requested 8,000 "captive Slavs" for work on reinforcing his positions. Two thousand were sent from the Kazan' POW camp and 6,000 from Omsk. Civilian authorities were granted permission to employ "captive Slavs" in agricultural work in Ekaterinoslav province. See Alon Rachamimov, *POWs and the Great War: Captivity on the Eastern Front* (Oxford and New York: Berg, 2002).

86. RGVIA, f. 2003, op. 2, d. 331, ll. 3–4. The Foreign Ministry letter to the War Ministry is dated 30 December 1915. RGVIA f. 2003, op. 2, d. 325, l. 10.

87. For a treatment of the first two decades of the twentieth-century rivalry that emphasizes the international dimensions, see chapter 8 in Eduard Winter, *Byzanz und Rom im Kampf um die Ukraine, 955–1939* (Leipzig: Otto Harrassowitz, 1942); for a brief English-language introduction, see Bohdan Rostyslav Bociurkiw, *The Ukrainian Greek Catholic Church and the Soviet State (1939–1950)* (Edmonton and Toronto: Canadian Institute of Ukrainian Studies Press, 1996), pp. 14–21.

88. Evlogii's address, "K galitsko-russkomu narodu i ego dukhovenstvu," was published in *Prikarpatskaia Rus'* (6 December 1914); both Evlogii's address and Sheptits'kyi's letter are cited in Bakhturina, *Politika*, pp. 142–143, 160, 170. Sheptits'kyi delivered a sermon on 6 September 1914 in which he contrasted the bureaucratic (*kazionne*, and implying a coerced or artificial character) faith of the Russians with the ecclesiastical orthodoxy of the holy Catholic Church. This sermon was deemed subversive by Russian authorities and was long thought to be the pretext for his arrest. Bakhturina (chapter 2) argues that the decision to arrest him had been taken long before and was intended to turn up documents in his archive incriminating him in a plot with the Pope and Austria-Hungary to annex Russian Ukraine.

89. For Evlogii's version of his experiences in Galicia, see his memoirs, *Put' moei zhizni*, pp. 253–255, 258–269.

90. Bakhturina, *Politika*, p. 144.

91. Bakhturina, ibid., pp. 151–152.

92. A second Greek-Catholic bishop died during the siege of Peremyshl; the third Galician bishop fled to Vienna. Within one month, and at a particularly critical moment in its history, the Greek Catholic Church was left without any leadership.

93. Bakhturina, *Politica*, pp. 144–151.

94. Ibid., p. 147, citing records of a conversation between Ianushkevich and the Interior Ministry's representative at Stavka, Prince N. Kudashev.

95. From Kiev, Sheptits'kyi was transferred under armed escort to Nizhnii Novogorod, then to Kursk, and finally to a monastery in Suzdal', where he remained until 1917. In his memoirs, Brusilov recalled his meeting with Sheptits'kyi. "The Uniate Metropolitan Count Sheptitskii, an obvious enemy of Russia who had for a long time constantly agitated against us, was subjected to house arrest as a preliminary measure on my orders as soon as Russian troops entered L'vov." A. A. Brusilov, *Moi vospominaniia* (Moscow: Voenizdat, 1983), p. 86.

96. Bakhturina, *Politika*, pp. 153–154. Foreign Minister Sazonov expressed alarm about the international diplomatic fallout over the arrest.

97. *Armeiskii vestnik* (2 October 1914), p. 4. Bociurkiw (*The Ukrainian Greek Catholic Church*, p. 68) cites the text of Bobrinskii's decree from *Tserkovnyi vestnik*: "The [military] authorities intend to show full religious tolerance, not to allow forcible conversions to Orthodoxy, [but] they will not permit the return from hiding of the Uniate and Catholic priests to their previous posts. . . New priests will not be admitted [to vacated parishes] without the special permission of the governor-general in each case; Orthodox priests should be sent to villages according to the wishes of the *inhabitants*, but only after three-fourths of them have expressed their wish to have, specifically, an Orthodox priest.. . . If there is a Uniate priest in the parish but three-fourths of the inhabitants would nevertheless prefer an Orthodox priest, the former shall remain in charge of the [local] church, while another building should be allocated for Orthodox services."

98. Bakhturina, *Politika*, pp. 162–165.

99. Oleh W. Gerus, "The Ukrainian Question in the Russia Dumas, 1906–1917: An Overview," *Studia Ucrainica* 2 (1984): 165–166. Grand Duke Nikolai Nikolaevich complained that the Russian officials in the newly occupied territories were so zealous in their efforts at the forcible conversion of Ukrainian Uniates to Orthodoxy that they commandeered desperately needed ammunitions trains to transport Orthodox priests to the region. Lincoln quotes Paleologue, *La Russie des Tsars*, I, pp. 222–223. Bobrinskii claimed that 86 Orthodox priests were appointed during the occupation months, whereas Evlogii counted 113 by April 1915. The statistics on conversion of ordinary believers to Orthodoxy are equally contested and problematic. During the nine months of occupation estimates, Evlogii claimed that 200 parishes had converted. The total prewar population of Uniates in Galicia was estimated at 3.5 million believers. Bakhturina, pp. 166–178.

100. "Otchet," RGVIA f. 2003, op. 2, d. 539, l. 80. Bobrinskii's criticism of Evlogii appears slightly disingenuous to judge from an interview he gave in April 1915 to *Russkoe slovo*, in which he admitted that Orthodox priests were being sent into vacated villages without a vote of the parishioners, but that "the Uniate Church has no future. An insignificant part of the Uniates will switch to [Roman] Catholicism, and the main mass [of them] will convert to Orthodoxy without any involvement on our part." Bociurkiw, *The Ukrainian Greek Catholic Church*, p. 17.

101. Shavel'skii claims he played a critical role in the tsar's decision to recall Evlogii; see his *Vospominaniia poslednego protopresvitera rossiiskoi armii i flota* (New York, 1954), pp. 180–181.

102. Bociukiw (*The Ukrainian Greek Catholic Church*, p. 17n) cites *Vsepoddaneishii doklad Ober-Prokuroru Sinoda ob ustroistve Pravoslavnoi Tserkvi v zavoevannoi Rossieiu chasti Galitsii* (Petrograd, 1915), pp. 15–16.

CHAPTER 3

The Ukrainian Adventure of the Central Powers [1]

German War Aims: The Separation of the *Randvoelker* of the Russian Empire

The general aim of the war . . . was security for the German Reich in west and east for all imaginable time. For this purpose France must be so weakened as to make her revival as a great power impossible for all time. Russia must be thrust back as far as possible from Germany's eastern frontier and her domination over the non-Russian vassal peoples broken.
– German Chancellor Bethmann Hollweg, 9 September 1914 [2]

The question is one of victory or extinction, not one of gain or loss in power or territory. If we win—and anyone who doubts we shall is a cur—we can impose our rules on the conquered world and give things the shape necessary for our own development and for the good of the small neighboring peoples that flock around us and look to us for protection and salvation.
— Johannes Haller, in *Sueddeutsche Monatshefte*, September 1914 [3]

FROM THE BEGINNING OF THE WAR the German and Austrian Foreign and War Ministries, in formulating their primary war aim of weakening Russian power both during the war and after, concurred that fomenting domestic unrest in the Russian Empire, particularly national uprisings and revolution, would be effective tactics. German officials were more committed to the subversive projects than their generally more cautious Austrian allies and eventually took over most of the activities when Vienna grew disenchanted with the Ukrainian nationalists and began to worry about the repercussions on its own ability to manage Polish-Ukrainian relations at home. Still, the Austrian Foreign Ministry remained more enthusiastic about the subversion projects than did the Austrian High Command. Even more enthusiastic advocates of the dismemberment of the Russian Empire through the uprisings of its *Randvoelker* (borderland peoples) were to be found in the Pan-German League and among Baltic German publicists and academic experts. [4] The plans, in their most moderate versions, envisioned the establishment of a ring of buffer states, including Poland and Ukraine, to keep Russia at a safer distance; but even these plans entailed inciting rebellions among the borderland peoples, either national or socialist. Especially after the 1905–06 revolutions in the Russian Empire, a considerable wave of emigration to Europe (and North America) created pockets of potential subversives who dreamed of bringing down the Romanov autocracy. Not only could the German government count on the conservative nationalist parties in their war aims of detaching Russia's "borderland peoples" from St. Petersburg, but also liberals, social-democrats, and even pacifists supported "the liberation of the non-Russian peoples" in the name of national self-determination and the protection of the rights of oppressed peoples from despotic, autocratic Russia. The first mention of the liberation of Poland is dated 5 August; of Finland 6 August, and Ukraine 11 August, in a message from the Chancellor to the German embassy in Vienna: "To produce revolution, not only in Poland, but also in Ukraine, seems to us very important." The Austrian Foreign Minister, in confidential communications with the Young Turk government at the beginning of November, argued that the Central Powers should "welcome the establishment of an independent Ukrainian State."[5]

The high point of Central Power support for the subversive activities of Ukrainian nationalists came at the end of 1914, after which official enthusiasm cooled, especially in Austrian circles. But for a few months a range of military and diplomatic bureaucrats in Berlin and Vienna conjured up various scenarios for revolutionary uprisings in the Russian Empire.[6] The most enthusiastic supporter of the subversive projects in the German Foreign Office was Undersecretary Arthur Zimmermann who, already in early August 1914, outlined plans for national revolutions in the border areas from Finland to the Caucasus. A second important official voice, in this case, for the creation of a Ukrainian buffer state as a democratic republic and based on land redistribution to the peasants, was that of Albrecht von Rechenberg, the Polish expert in the Foreign Ministry.[7] Still, the diverse agendas that were pursued in Vienna, Berlin, Lemberg, and other sites often worked at cross-purposes in the absence of any genuinely coordinated or well-prepared plans, and during the first period of the war remained of an improvised and ad hoc character.[8]

The first contacts between the Central Powers and the Ukrainian politicians were made through their diplomatic representatives in Lemberg; simultaneously, the Ukrainian Parliamentary Club (Kost' Levyts'kyi and Mykola Vasylko) in Vienna made contacts with German and Austrian officials there. The Austrian Foreign Ministry appointed Emanuel Urbas as special consul for Ukrainian affairs and dispatched him to Lemberg within days after the declaration of war to meet with representatives of the major Austrian and Russian Ukrainian parties; he was joined by the German consul general in Lemberg, Karl Heinze. Those discussions, many of which took place in the residential palace of the Metropolitan of Galicia, Andrei Sheptits'kyi, included the issue of War Ministry financing for "a volunteer Ukrainian legion." The Metropolitan acted as the leader of the Ukrainian nation during these weeks and was perceived as such by both Austrian and Russian authorities. But sharp differences quickly emerged between the rival visions of Ukraine that were held by the more conservative Austrian Ukrainian politicians who dominated the Ukrainian National Council and their more radical Russian Ukrainian émigré counterparts in ULU. Levyts'kyi and Vasylko hoped to wrest from Vienna the designation of eastern Galicia and Bukovyna as an autonomous crownland free from Polish dominance, whereas Marian Melenevsk'yi and Aleksandr Skoropis-Ioltukhovs'kyi advocated social revolution and the creation of a democratic, independent Ukraine on formerly Russian territory. The leaders of ULU offered to fight for the Central Powers against Russia in order to help incite uprisings in Russian Ukraine after the entry of German and Austrian armies there, and stressed the urgency of agrarian reform to win over the Ukrainian population. Moreover, ULU promised to recruit new members among Russian-Ukrainian émigrés in Italy, Sweden, and Switzerland, and to train these new members with the aim of sending them back into Russian Ukraine to serve the aims of the Union, including fomenting revolution against the Russian autocracy. They promised to conduct extensive work for the "political and national enlightenment of the people" and to cultivate support for the Austrian and German armies.[9] The two groups were, however, able to agree on the need for the Central Powers to support the "Ukrainian Free Legions," and won quick approval for their proposals. During the war years, Austrian and German officials frequently tried to reconcile these two approaches for unified action against Russia, but almost as often found themselves being played off one another by the Ukrainian activists. Over time, ULU emerged as the most influential Ukrainian organization on the Central Powers' policies; importantly, ULU became the first Ukrainian organization to bring together representatives of all major groups in Galicia, Bukovyna, and Russian Ukraine for active cooperation in promoting an independent Ukrainian state.

When the Russians began their invasion of Galicia, the émigrés quickly moved to Vienna and founded a branch in Berlin as well, where they enjoyed the limited financial and political support of both Germany and Austria. With the initial intentions of the Central Powers to use ULU in occupied areas of southern Russia rendered temporarily moot by the Russian military successes, the main focus of their activities was to publicize the Ukrainian cause, in Vienna and the international community more generally. Indeed, ULU evolved into a proto-diplomatic corps and press and information agency with representatives in several capitals deemed potentially friendly to the Ukrainian cause.[10] The Austrian Foreign Ministry, to convince their German allies of their support for the anti-Russian subversion effort, issued an "appeal to the public conscience of Europe" for solidarity with the Ukrainians' determination to defend their nation from Russia.[11]

Soon the Austrians began to grow wary in their contacts with and control over ULU, especially after reports reached the Foreign Ministry (from the German ambassador in Vienna) that ULU propaganda had created considerable support among Austria's Ruthenians for the idea of union with a future Russian-Ukrainian state, a prospect not greeted warmly by the Austrian authorities who continued to worry about their relations with "their" Poles. On 10 January 1915, the Foreign Ministry insisted that the Ukrainians cease their activities and sever relations with Ukrainians on the territory of the Dual Monarchy and move their headquarters to the capital of another allied power, Constantinople, or to a neutral country, such as Switzerland.[12] (Turkey entered the war on the side of the Central Powers against Russia on 29 October.) ULU leaders had tried to argue against the move to Turkey as sending the wrong signal to the Ukrainian movement at a time when encouraging signs of the success of ULU propaganda were at hand. (Skoropys-Zholtukhovs'kyi reported that 700 Kuban' Cossacks had been arrested by their own Russian superiors in eastern Galicia for refusing to fight against their Ukrainian brothers in the Austrian army.)[13] The move to Turkey also marked the definitive ascendance of Germany over Austria in support for ULU, because Germany's relations with the Porte were much closer and more extensive. Accordingly, ULU also kept an important office in Berlin as a liaison with German military and diplomatic officials.[14] ULU, like many other organizations devoted to national liberation, engaged in extensive diplomatic activity with the Central Powers throughout the war. In addition, and somewhat at cross-purposes, Petro Chykalenko conducted antiwar activities in Stockholm in the summer and fall of 1916; Volodymyr

Temnyts'kyi attended the International Socialist Conference in Stockholm in June 1917. Among the most ambitious of ULU's activities were the efforts to win the favor of the Turkish government. ULU proposed collaboration with various Turkic and Muslim émigré organizations for joint action against the Russian Empire; beyond that, ULU suggested that the Ukrainian Sharpshooters join with Turkish forces in joint military campaigns.[15] These activities aroused concern among other groups of Ukrainians, especially several in Switzerland and Ukrainians remaining in Russia.[16]

It was also in Constantinople that ULU made its first contacts with Bolshevik agents; Melenevs'kyi met with Alexander Helphand (Parvus) and transferred German funds through him to the Bolshevik Party. Likewise, in Sofia, ULU's agent there had more direct contacts with Lenin.[17] These contacts were encouraged by the Germans, who, during the winter of December 1914–15, had gradually shifted their interest from inciting national uprisings toward a socialist revolution; the Ukrainians were urged to join efforts in a unified socialist front. Among the other non-Russian socialists active in forging this front was the Estonian Socialist Alexander Keskuela, who was also a member of the Estonian National Committee.[18]

Fairly early in the Austro-German-Ukrainian collaboration, the parties arrived at a vague division of labor between the rival Ukrainian organizations. That division was quickly tested when the Austrian and German armies reversed the Russian advances of the fall of 1914 during their spring–summer offensive in 1915. The Ukrainian National Council had primary responsibility for countering the Russification policies of the occupation regime in Galicia and Bukovyna, whereas the Union for the Liberation of Ukraine was assigned work in Ukrainian areas of Russia occupied by German and Austrian armies during the 1915–1916 campaigns, and were granted permission by Austrian authorities to conduct propaganda work and recruitment in the prisoner-of-war camps for captured soldiers of the Russian Army. Melenevs'kyi persuaded the Central Powers that an ULU-administered occupied Ukraine could build the foundations for a provisional government for the postwar period. In June 1915 ULU and the Ukrainian National Council even joined forces formally in the General Ukrainian National Council (*Zahal'na Ukrains'ka Narodova Rada*) with the common goals of a free and independent Ukrainian state in southern Russia and the creation of a Ukrainian crownland in the Habsburg empire based on national-territorial autonomy and democracy. ULU was committed to an independent Ukrainian state and remained active until a Ukrainian state allied to the Central Powers was established in the spring of 1918.[19] Once the United States entered the war and President Wilson began his efforts to convene an international peace conference, ULU representatives turned to him and insisted that they had the right to represent the interests of all Russian Ukrainians at any future conference.[20]

The German/Austrian Reoccupation of Galicia and Russian Ukraine/Poland: The Politics of Austria's Ukrainian Piedmont Project

Following the Austrian reconquest of Galicia, a new occupation regime began to quickly supplant the Russian institutions and personnel. German rhetoric in particular bore a striking resemblance to the slogans of the recently departed Russian Army as the "liberator" of oppressed nationalities. German Chancellor Bethmann Hollweg proclaimed to the Reichstag that "we, with our allies, have liberated almost all Galicia and Poland, we have liberated Lithuania and Courland from the Russians."[21] But now the scorched-earth policy of the retreating Russians posed formidable challenges to the administrators of this ravaged territory and its brutalized remaining population. The Central Powers' advances brought Congress Poland, the Russian-ruled partition territories, under their authority. The politics of a future Polish state brought to the surface contradictory interests within the Austrian bureaucracy and, before long, between the German and Austrian wartime allies. The coming conflict was institutionalized in the creation of two separate military administrations for Poland and the lands to the east. On 25 July the Germans created the General Gouvernement of Warsaw; the Austrian Army Administration set up its headquarters in Lublin. These two occupation regimes would serve as the allies' respective models for a future Poland more closely associated with one than the other. The struggle over Poland's future was inextricably tied to the emerging rival visions for a Ukrainian buffer state; the Polish factor served at various times either to constrain or offer opportunities for Ukrainian elites.

In August 1915 Kost' Levyts'kyi protested—on behalf of the General Ukrainian National Council but in the name of the entire Ukrainian nation in Austria and Russia—to a new Austrian Foreign Minister, Count Stefan Burian, against the inclusion of the newly occupied Kholm district in the Austrian military district of Poland (*Militaergeneralgouvernement Lublin*). He marshaled considerable demographic evidence to claim that Ukrainian territory extended over 775,000 square kilometers, on which 40 million

Ukrainians lived. He argued that a Ukrainian state would serve the interests of Germany, Austria-Hungary, and their Turkish allies by cutting off Russia from the Black Sea and the Balkans and thereby diminishing Russia's overall threat to Europe. He offered a vision of Ukraine as a dam against the wave of Russian-dominated Pan-Slavism that threatened to wash over Europe. He warned that Polish politicians falsely counted hundreds of thousands of Ukrainians as Poles by falsifying their statistics. But given the choice between Poland and Russia, this large population would most likely prefer Russia; therefore, any policies that overly favored Poles over Ukrainians would incline the Ukrainians to view the Russians as their liberators in the next military campaign.[22] The foreign minister felt himself constrained by Austrian promises to Polish elites and refused, whereas his ambassador in Berlin, Prince Gottfried zu Hohenlohe-Langenburg, pushed forward a proposal to separate East Galicia from any future Poland and to unite it with Bukovyna in a separate crownland in the Dual Monarchy as an attractive example for Ukrainians in the Russian Empire—and potentially encouraging their secession. Here was the nucleus of an Austrian-sponsored nation-building project with the Galician experience of Ukrainian cultural rights as the Piedmont from which these principles would be extended into occupied Russian territory.[23] Still, the 14 September 1915 announcement from Army press headquarters on the creation of the Lublin military general governorship forced the Ukrainians to realize their weak position on this matter. Repeated appeals from ULU and the Ukrainian National Council met with similar rejections.[24]

The Germans encouraged the Piedmont policy, especially after their repeated disappointments in winning Russia over to a separate peace reinforced those who spoke for the greater project of dismantling the Russian Empire. Chancellor Bethmann Hollweg endorsed the program of detaching the "borderland peoples" from the Russian core in a report to Emperor Wilhelm: "Should the military developments and events in Russia itself make it possible *to thrust the Muscovite Empire back eastward, detaching its western portions,* then our liberation from this nightmare in the east would certainly be a worthwhile goal, worth the great sacrifices and extraordinary exertions of this war."[25] Publicists and professors encouraged such liberationist thinking and provided the scholarly buttressing for these ambitions with their writings about the Russian Empire. Typical was Theodor Schiemann, of Baltic German origins, who denied the organic nature of the Russian state and insisted instead that it be seen as "a conglomerate of peoples held together artificially by the iron vice of a monarchy which had degenerated into despotism." From that vision, he demanded the right of secession for the oppressed peoples from Russia.[26] These German aims were entrusted in spring 1916 to the League of Russia's Foreign Peoples, which originally brought together representatives of the Russian Empire's Jews, Mohammedans, Georgians, Poles, Baltic Germans, Finns, and Ukrainians to coordinate their revolutionary activities with Foreign Ministry support.[27] The political arrangements for the projected belt of buffer states between Russia and Germany remained vague; they often involved "native" princes ruling over the liberated territories, but also envisioned deportations of the "native" populations and their replacement with German settlers.[28] In a characterization of Germans that had its analogue in the writings of Russian historian Vasilii Kliuchevskii, Friedrich von Schwerin, President of the Society for the Promotion of Internal Colonization, appealed to "the German people, the greatest colonizing people of the world" to be "mobilized again for a great operation of colonization." The lands Schwerin targeted for the Germans' *Lebensraum* lay to the east of the current German borders.[29]

In a similar vein, the German Foreign Minister, Gottlieb von Jagow, embellished his appeals to his Austrian counterpart with the rhetoric of Germanic unity against the Slavic menace; for Jagow, Russia was excluded from European civilization by its racial and cultural features. For such men, resurrecting a Polish state was tolerable only because the Poles, though Slavs, separated from Orthodox Russians by their Catholic and Protestant religions. But in Jagow's ambitious visions, Austria-Hungary would merge with a greater Germany as the Germanic Eastern March, a projection of Germanic influence into the Slavic world. The Germans' acceptance of an Austro-Poland came with insistence that Germany be the real master of the newly "independent" state. In fact, the Austrians had little choice but to accommodate to their powerful German allies' plans for reshaping East Central and Eastern Europe; the futility of occasional protests led to an increasing sense of fatalistic resignation to changes that were clearly not always in the best interests of the Dual Monarchy.[30]

The Ukrainians appealed to Vienna and, increasingly, to Berlin with the arguments that Russian authorities had trampled on the linguistic and religious freedoms of Ukrainians for nearly a century and, in effect, called for the Austrian military authorities to recognize the Russian government's detachment of Kholm in 1912; ironically, this campaign had been spearheaded by the Ukrainians' bitterest rivals in Russia, Vladimir Bobrinskii and Bishop Evlogii. They buttressed their claims with ethnographic data, which the Foreign Ministry's experts disputed with their own data showing more ethnic Poles than the Ukrainians claimed for the district.[31] In Levyts'kyi's August 1915 memorandum to the Austrian War Ministry, he proposed the outlines of an occupation policy for the newly conquered territories, as well as those remaining parts of the Russian Empire that might be liberated by the armies of the Central Powers in future advances. Borrowing from the platform of ULU, he emphasized the urgency of addressing the land shortage among Ukrainian peasants with a combination of redistribution and resettlement. Such timely interventions would secure the loyalties of a basically conservative Ukrainian peasantry. He also called for a restoration of an autocephalous Ukrainian Orthodox Church, but warned that the clergy currently administering to the spiritual needs of Ukrainians was mostly imported from Great Russia and would resist such moves toward independence from the Holy Synod. Levyts'kyi also assured the Central Powers that despite the Russian authorities' forcible removal of much of the Ukrainian intelligentsia, there were nonetheless large numbers of concealed Ukrainian nationalists among the urban educated classes and bureaucracy and that one could even expect Russified merchants and industrialists to come to appreciate the advantages of independence for their own position. In short, Ukraine had the potential to become a viable state, if Central Powers policies were wisely crafted and implemented. Those policies should be proclaimed in the Ukrainian language and needed to promise equality for all nations. If the occupying authorities could be persuaded that Ukraine was not Russia and that Ukrainians were not necessarily hostile to them, they would quickly win over the local population. Levyts'kyi urged that the occupying authorities hire Ukrainian translators and informants to counter the tendentious information about Ukrainian matters that came from hostile Jews and Poles. He raised the issue from prewar Galician politics of the creation of a Ukrainian university in Lemberg; such a symbolic gesture was even more important to counter the "widespread rumors of mass arrests and executions of Ukrainians in Austria." He called for expanding the number of Ukrainian legions and their deployment in Russian Ukraine, where they might also recruit from the local population into their ranks. Finally, he called for Ukrainian newspapers and schools to be established in the occupied regions and offered the services of his General Ukrainian National Council's membership.[32]

The Austrian High Command was ready to agree to accept Ukrainian translators, but less inclined to employ informants of Ukrainian ancestry; they rejected the expansion of the Ukrainian legion but allowed for native Ukrainians to enter the Imperial and Royal Army as volunteers if they so chose. The opening of newspapers was to be sanctioned, but without any state funding. Occupation authorities would make every effort to find civil bureaucrats proficient in the "Ruthenian" language, but no commitment was made to a Ukrainian university or to any appeals to the Ukrainian population in the Ukrainian language. The Central Powers ignored Levyts'kyi's most important proposal and proceeded to administer the new territories from the Lublin military general-governor's headquarters, refusing to antagonize their Polish subjects by raising their suspicions about a future Polish state.

Though many of Levyts'kyi's most important proposals for a pro-Ukrainian occupation regime were rejected,[33] his and ULU's constant political activity began to show results in actual practice. On 14 September 1915, the Austrians announced the principles of their occupation regime in Galicia. The new Austrian Governor-General, Major-General Erich Freiherr von Diller, recognized the claims made for use of the Ukrainian language and declared that the Ukrainian language would be reintroduced for local administration. But after ULU activists had pressed the new occupiers for prominent positions for their own members, Diller alarmed ULU leaders by appointing many Poles to the new regime.[34] Three officers from the Ukrainian Legion were assigned to recruit volunteers in occupied Volynia for the Austrian Army. ULU requested that the Ukrainian Legion be enlarged to 12,000 active duty and 5,000 reservists, with an eye to the future liberation struggle. They also asked for the creation of special officers' and NCO schools for the Legion and the appointment of a Ukrainian officer as liaison (*Hilfsreferent*) to the Army High Command. The ULU's geopolitical vision can be characterized by the suggestion that the volunteer formation from Bukovyna, the Ruthenische-Huzulen-Freiwilliger Korps, be merged with the Ukrainian Legion and accordingly renamed as the *Bukowinaer Regiment der K.K. ukrainischer Legion*.[35] In effect, the Austrians and Germans were being drawn, largely unwittingly, into the nation-building politics not only of the Ukrainians, but also of the Poles and others. The German Governor-General of Warsaw, General Hans von Beseler, became one of the most ardent advocates of an independent Polish state because he saw such a state as a partial solution to Austria's manpower shortages. He argued that a military service law in an independent Polish state allied with the Central Powers would provide more troops than the current reliance on volunteer recruiting to the Polish Legions could yield. The Germans desperately looked to Poland to possibly recruit 900,000 to 1 million soldiers. Despite the rejection of this rationale by von Beseler's military superiors, by November 1916 the two Emperors finally agreed to a vague statement about a future, independent Poland, albeit without a regular army.[36] A similar logic allowed the Central Powers to tolerate the military and paramilitary activities of ULU among Ukrainians.

The other most important nation- and state-building activities sanctioned by the occupying authorities were in the realms of schools, religious politics, and newspaper publishing. In one of several analytic memoranda on religious matters, the presidium of the General Ukrainian National Council appealed to the Austrian authorities to uphold the international Hague conventions, in contrast to the Russian Army's occupation policy, and to defend religious freedom and tolerance, arguing that in so doing the occupation authorities stood a good chance to win the confidence of the local population. The Council defined religious freedom as, among other items, the restoration of the Union of Brest and the Uniate Church in areas where Russian authorities had banned the Union and persecuted its adherents. A Greek-Catholic diocese should be created for Kholm province and Galician priests—preferably patriotic but moderate and tolerant—should be assigned to the region. Again, in dramatic contrast to the Russian policies, no Orthodox churches or monasteries ought to be forcibly confiscated and transferred to Greek-Catholic parishes; instead, the presidium recommended gradual Ukrainianization of the Orthodox Church with an aim to establish an autocephalous organization, independent of the oversight of the Holy Synod in Petrograd. Because of the large-scale exodus of Orthodox clergy with the retreating Russian Army, Ukrainian Orthodox priests from Bukovyna were to be sent to Kholm to replace them. Those priests would be subordinate provisionally to the Orthodox consistory in Czernowitz, the seat of the Church in Austria-Hungary. Besides Greek-Catholic and Ukrainian Orthodox churches, the proposals for religious tolerance extended to Roman-Catholic clergy and parishioners as well. The failure of the Austrian High Command to act on these proposals led to another appeal over two months later from the Ukrainian politicians.[37]

ULU and the Ukrainian National Council drafted similar recommendations on school policy in the occupied territories; these began with a politic expression of gratitude to the Austrian High Command for recognizing Ukrainian as the language of instruction in Ukrainian cities and villages. (The AOK decreed the introduction of Ukrainian language in schools and self-administration of all Ukrainian schools on 17 October 1915.) The Russian deportation of the Ukrainian intelligentsia from the region, especially schoolteachers, required that replacement schoolteachers be sent from Galicia and Bukovyna to organize and administer the Ukrainian schools. The Ukrainians requested permission for some of their most prominent intellectuals to enter the occupied lands, including the historian Ivan Krypakiewicz, who had been born in Kholm; Andrii Zhuk, also from Russian Ukraine but with extensive experience in founding private Ukrainian schools and cooperatives in prewar eastern Galicia and a founding member of ULU; and Ivan Kossak, gymnasium teacher and veteran of the Ukrainian legion. Subsequent memoranda stressed the importance of schools for cultivating the nation, recalled the history of Russification efforts through the schools in prewar Ukraine, and even suggested that Austrian authorities, in contrast to their Russian counterparts, would be in fact implementing a recommendation accepted by the all-Russian pedagogical congress in Moscow in 1913 that schools in Ukraine be Ukrainianized. Finally, for those teachers who had not fled with the retreating Russian armies, special short courses would be organized to familiarize them with the principles of Austrian and Ukrainian schools; stipends would allow these teachers to attend courses in Galicia. As the crown of this edifice of educational reforms, the Ukrainians once again raised their request for a Ukrainian university in Lemberg as an important symbolic gesture for Ukrainians in the Russian Empire.[38]

When, in March 1916, a formal response finally came from the Foreign Minister, it proved disappointing to the Ukrainians. Burian interpreted the Ukrainian proposals in the spirit of their campaign to detach Kholm and other occupied regions from Polish-dominated Galicia as part of a "Little Russian" district and historic Ukrainian lands. He reminded his representative at AOK that any such distinctively Ukrainian school administration plans would be understood by Poles as accepting the detachment of these lands from any future Poland. In light of this anticipated response, Burian recommended extreme caution in turning over Russian schools in Kholm to the Ruthenians, although he was more willing to countenance such wholesale Ukrainianization in Volynia. In line with vague plans to annex Volynia to eastern Galicia and to integrate these lands into Austrian administrative frameworks, the Foreign Minister agreed to the proposals to send Galician school personnel to Volynia, especially those with a mastery of the Ukrainian language. Financial considerations, however, dictated a delay in plans for building any new Ukrainian schools in the occupied territories, instead directing support to existing private schools there.[39]

ULU also requested permission to publish the first anti-Russian, pro-Austro-Hungarian Ukrainian newspaper on Russian territory. Claiming that the Russian government had closed nearly twenty Ukrainian newspapers since the outbreak of the war, ULU argued that a newspaper would help counter the false and mistaken impressions about the flight of the Ukrainian population in Volynia from the advancing Austro-Hungarian army and help win over the remaining population to the cause of liberating Ukraine from Russia. The Austrian High Command was able to approve this request on both "military and political grounds."[40]

In the spheres of educational, religious, press, and military policy, Ukrainian politicians appealed to the Austrian authorities with proposals to extend essentially Austrian administrative practice to the newly conquered and occupied lands as a model for a future Austro-Ukrainian state. All these activities were designed to shore up their increasingly shaky position with their would-be allies, who did show renewed interest in their activities with the Russian retreat and Austrian-German victories. At the end of 1915, ULU renewed its request to Austria and Germany to openly declare itself in favor of Ukrainian independence. No such declaration was forthcoming, though a more lukewarm endorsement of ULU was approved.[41] A ULU delegation complained to the Hungarian Minister-President Count Tisza that the Monarchy's policies had taken an anti-Ukrainian coloring of late and feared that the Hungarian government was willing to hand over Galicia to the Poles; moreover, Andrii Zhuk forwarded to the Austrians complaints that Volynia had been "liberated" from the Russians only to be delivered into the hands of Poles, who dominated among the Austrian occupation regime's key positions.[42] The Declaration of Polish Statehood fanned those fears the following year.[43] In response to the Polish Declaration of Statehood in November 1916 and the German-Austrian declaration of support, ULU distributed a questionnaire among POWs to ascertain their attitude to the declaration. Following the collection of the questionnaires, a 252-man meeting passed a resolution protesting "any decisions about Ukrainian lands (or any part thereof)" without the will and agreement of the Ukrainian people. In particular, the participants protested against the Polish declaration and its provision for call-up of citizens into a Polish national army. They declared, "Ukrainians can only fight in their own army, for history has taught us not to expect anything good from either Russia or Poland." They sent a warning to the Central Powers that should the Russian Empire collapse, but part of Ukraine fall to Poland (Kholm, Polisia, Volynia), they could expect "new catastrophes." They petitioned the Austrian authorities to administer these lands separately from Poland during the occupation period. The greatest influence of ULU propaganda on the resolution was contained in the declaration of intent, in the event that the war does not bring about the collapse of Russia, to form a separate crown land tied to the Central Powers, but in no way to Poland.[44]

NOTES

1. This title is taken from an unpublished dissertation of the same name by Jerry Hans Hoffman (Ph.D. dissertation, University of Pittsburgh, 1967); Hoffman's study is the major English-language treatment of German and Austrian policies toward Ukraine and is based on Foreign and War Ministry archives in Berlin and Vienna.
2. Cited in Fritz Fischer, Germany's Aims, p. 103.
3. Cited in Fritz Fischer, World Power or Decline: The Controversy over "Germany's Aims in the First World War" (New York: Norton, 1974), p. 1.
4. For more on the official and unofficial interest groups promoting Germany's policies toward Russia's national minorities, see Fischer, Germany's Aims, pp. 122–126; 132–154; and chapter 5. In the Foreign Ministry, Fischer identifies Arthur Zimmermann, Rudolf Nadolny, Baron Uexkill, and Diego von Bergen as the key players; another key government player was Friedrich von Schwerin; outside of the government Theodor Schiemann, Paul Rohrbach, and Johannes Haller served as advisors and propagandists for the German cause. On the Pan-German League and other radical nationalists, see Geoff Eley, Reshaping the German Right: Radical Nationalism and Political Change after Bismarck (New Haven, CT: Yale University Press, 1980).
5. Fischer, Germany's Aims, p. 132–134. Hoffman also records German Emperor Wilhelm II's approval of the insurgency activities in Ukraine, Finland, Poland, and the Caucasus on 8 August; see "The Ukrainian Adventure," pp. 16, 21. On background to the German and Austrian plans for Ukraine, see Hoffman, "The Ukrainian Adventure of the Central Powers, 1914–1918," chapter 1. See also Austrian Foreign Ministry correspondence with ambassadors in Constantinople and Berlin, "Ueber das angestrebte Hauptziel der oest-ung. Monarchie in bezug auf die Schwaechung Russlands durch Gruendung eines unabhaengigen ukrain. Staates," 20 November 1914; on ULU contacts with Turkey's Interior Minister, "Ueber die Kontakte des Bundes z. B. d. U. mit Talaat Bey," 1 December 1914, in Hornykiewicz, Ereignisse, I, pp. 168–170.

6. See ULU's report of its propaganda and subversive activities for September–December 1914 in "Bericht ueber die organisatorische, literarisch-informative und aufklaerende Taetigkeit des Bundes in Oesterreich und im Auslande fuer die Zeit September–Dezember 1914, Zusammenstellung der Kosten," 16 December 1914, in Hornykiewicz, *Ereignisse*, I, pp. 170–190.

7. Hoffman discusses an important memorandum written by Rechenberg for an undersecretary in the chancellery, dated 2 September 1914; see "The Ukrainian Adventure," pp. 27–28.

8. On the Union, Austria and Germany during the war, see Oleh S. Fedyshyn, "The Germans and the Union for the Liberation of the Ukraine, 1914–1917," in Hunczak, ed., *The Ukraine, 1917–1921: A Study in Revolution*, pp. 305–322; and Fedyshyn, *Germany's Drive to the East and the Ukrainian Revolution in World War I* (New Brunswick, NJ: Rutgers University Press, 1970), especially chapters I–III; and Helga Grebing, "Oesterreich-Ungarn und die 'Ukrainische Aktion' 1914–18," *Jahrbuecher fuer Geschichte Osteuropas*, N.F., VII, 3 (Munich, 1959), pp. 270–296. Fischer calculated that of the 382 million marks spent by the Germans on propaganda and special activities, nearly one-tenth of the funds, variously estimated at between 40 to 80 million marks, went to Ukrainian activities. *Germany's Aims*, p. 153n. For ULU's history, see Gregory Smolynec, "The Union for the Liberation of Ukraine, 1914–1918" (Master's thesis, Carleton University, 1993).

9. See report from Urbas in Lemberg, "Ueber den Bund z. B. d. U., ueber die Wichtigkeit der Loesung der Agrarfrage in der russ. Ukr. Und ueber die propagandistische Aufrufe des genannten Bundes," 1 September 1914; "Ueber die Ziele des Bundes, sein Verhaeltnis zum Allg. Ukr. N-Rat und sein Bestreben, die Unterstuetzung der oesterreichischen Regierung zu erlangen," 7 September 1914; and "Information ueber die beabsichtigte Taetigkeit des Bundes z. B. d. U.," no date; in Hornykiewicz, *Ereignisse*, I, pp. 160–165.

10. Russian military intelligence was aware that Ukrainians had organized special political agencies (*agentstva*) in Rome, Copenhagen, the Hague, Bucharest, Sofia, and Constantinople, whose purpose was to popularize the Ukrainian cause. RGVIA f. 2003, op. 2, d. 1018, l. 309. On Austria's relations with the Ukrainian movement, see Wolfdieter Bihl, "Einige Aspekte der oesterreichisch-ungarischen Ruthenenpolitik 1914–1918," *Jahrbuecher fuer Geschichte Osteuropas*, N.F., XIV (Wiesbaden, 1966), pp. 539–550.

11. Hoffman, "The Ukrainian Adventure," pp. 52–58.

12. On the Austrian government's quiet decision to "loosen its contacts" with the Ukrainian groups, see Hoffman, op. cit., pp. 63–65; see also the Foreign Ministry correspondence with ULU on a new basis for their relations in Hornykiewicz, *Ereignisse*, I, pp. 195–202.

13. "Ueber die 'Konstantinopler Aktion', die Rolle der ukrain. Intelligenz in der russ. Ukraine und Stellungnahme zur eventuellen Verlegung des Sitzes des Praesidiums des Bundes z. B. d. U. nach Konstantinopel," 20 December 1914, in Hornykiewicz, *Ereignisse*, I, pp. 191–195.

14. On ULU's reorientation from Vienna to Berlin, see documents dated 15 February and 13 March 1915, in Hornykiewicz, *Ereignisse*, I, pp. 202–206.

15. "Expedition to Turkey," 16 December 1914, Zhuk collection, vol. 8, file 7. ULU made contact with the *Komitet po okhraneniiu prav magometanskogo tiurksko-tatarskogo naseleniia Rossii.* See Zhuk collection, vol. 8, file 9. During October and November 1914, Austrian officials were in communication with Turkey about plans to offer Ukrainian volunteers to participate in the Turkish campaign against the Russian Caucasus and Kuban' region; the volunteers were to land on the coast of the Black Sea and raise a revolutionary movement in Ukraine. See Hornykiewicz, *Ereignisse,* I, pp. 144–159. See more below.

16. Doroshenko, in his *Moi spomyny,* recalls that upon learning of ULU's activities in Vienna, he warned them of the dangers of ULU being perceived as in the service of the Austrian General Staff, chapter i (L'viv), pp. 28–29. The differences in orientation toward Russia triggered a split within Ukrainian SDRP, with one faction (*Borot'ba*) choosing to emphasize opposition to autocracy over opposition to Russia itself. Zhuk collection, vol. 8. In Bern, Vladimir Stepankivsky set up a Ukrainian Bureau to publish French- and English-language newspapers on Ukrainian affairs and was eventually placed on the German payroll. Stepankivsky also was not above appealing to the Entente powers and had high hopes especially for Britain's eventual advocacy of independence not only for Ukrainians but also for Finns, Estonians, and others. Hoffman, "The Ukrainian Adventure," pp. 114–117.

17. See ULU's summary of its activities for the final quarter of 1914 in "Bericht," ibid., in Hornykiewicz, *Ereignisse,* I, p. 183.

18. Hoffman, "The Ukrainian Adventure," pp. 57–59, 77–83; Z. Zeman, *Germany and the Revolution in Russia* (London: Oxford University Press, 1958), pp. 1–24.

19. Ibid., pp. 90–93.

20. "Ukraine and Wilson's peace plans," Zhuk collection, vol. 10, file 16.

21. 19 August 1915, quoted in Fritz Fischer, *Germany's Aims,* p. 199.

22. "Denkschrift des Allg. Ukr. N-Rates an das k. u. k. Kriegsministerium ueber die Massnahmen zur Loesung der ukrain. Frage auf dem Gebiet der russ. Ukraine und Verwahrung gegen eventuelle Angliederung Ostgaliziens sowie neueroberten ukrain. Gebiete an Polen," Hornykiewicz, *Ereignisse,* I, pp. 84–92. For another representative defense of the historic distinctiveness of the Ukrainian lands from Poland, see a lead article, dated 14 October 1915, from the newspaper *Dilo* (published in Lemberg) translated for the Austrian Foreign Ministry, in Hornykiewicz, op. cit., pp. 94–97.

23. Fischer, *Germany's Aims,* p. 199.

24. See protests against inclusion of Kholm in the Polish General Gouvernement and Foreign Ministry responses, dated July and August 1916, in Hornykiewicz, *Ereignisse,* I, pp. 122–128. The AOK reaffirmed Austria's position on the inclusion of Kholm and the Grubieszow and Tomaszow districts in the Lublin Military General Gouvernement on 21 July 1916.

25. Quoted in Fischer, *Germany's Aims,* p. 198; according to Fischer, the Chancellor's report was written under the strong influence of Germany's ambassador in Copenhagen, Count Ulrich von Brockdorff-Rantzau (later Ambassador of Weimar Germany to Soviet Russia). Emphasis in the original.

26. Fischer, ibid, p. 275; see also Klaus Meyer, *Theodor Schiemann als Publizist* (Frankfurt am Main: Rütten & Loening, 1956).

27. Ibid., p. 237 footnote; see also Seppo Zetterberg, *Die Liga der Fremdvoelker Russlands 1916–1918. Ein Beitrag zu Deutschlands antirussischen Propagandakrieg unter den fremdvoelkern Russlands im ersten Weltkrieg* (Helsinki: Finnish Historical Society, 1978).

28. Fischer describes as representative of such projects that of Prince John Albert of Mecklenburg, President of the German Colonial Association and later Honorary President of the *Vaterlandspartei. Germany's Aims*, p. 182.

29. Fischer, *Germany's Aims*, pp. 162–163. Fischer sees Schwerin's ideas as having a great influence over Chancellor Bethmann Hollweg as his war aims evolved over the war years.

30. See Fischer's account of discussions between the foreign ministers of Germany and Austria-Hungary in *Germany's Aims*, pp. 202–212, 236–244. During the spring of 1916 Austrian Foreign Minister Burian suggested the creation of an autonomous Poland, including Kholm and parts of Volynia, within Austria's eventual customs zone; however, Jagow intended to establish an autonomous Poland, including formerly Austrian Galicia, under German suzerainty. He was supported in this plan by the German Governor-General in Warsaw, General Hans von Beseler. All these plans were put on hold when the Russian Army began what became known as the Brusilov offensive in June 1916.

31. Hoffman, "The Ukrainian Adventure," pp. 94–95; Hornykiewicz, *Ereignisse*, I, pp. 122–128. The Foreign Ministry's representative at AOK countered that the dominant population in the disputed territory was Polish; the non-Polish population had either departed with the enemy or were largely illiterate, not aware of their national affiliation, and used the Polish language.

32. "Denkschrift des Allg. Ukr. N-Rates," August 1915, in Hornykiewicz, *Ereignisse*, I, pp. 84–92.

33. "Stellungnahme des AOK zu den in obiger Denkschrift des Allg. Ukr. N-Rates enthaltenen Vorschlaegen," 30 August 1915, in Hornykiewicz, *Ereignisse*, I, pp. 92–93.

34. "Occupation of Cholm and Volyn," Zhuk collection, vol. 13, file 5. ULU petitioned Austrian authorities to open Ukrainian schools and appoint Ukrainians to the local police force. "Situation in Ukraine (occupied areas)," Zhuk collection, vol. 13, file 7. See also the adaptations of the general occupation regime guidelines for regions inhabited by Ukrainians: "Ueber die oesterreichische Nationalpolitik im Okkupationsgebiete und Gebrauch der ukrain. Sprache in Wort und Schrift im Verkehr mit der ukrain. Bevoelkerung dieses Gebietes," 18 September 1915, in Hornykiewicz, *Ereignisse*, I, pp. 93–94.

35. "Situation in Ukraine," Zhuk collection, vol. 13, file 7.

36. Fischer, *Germany's Aims*, pp. 243–245, 272.

37. "Denkschrift des Allgemeinen ukrainischen Nationalrates ueber die National- und Religionsfrage in Cholmland," 29 October 1915, and second appeal, 11 January 1916, in Hornykiewicz, *Ereignisse*, I, pp. 97–109.

38. "Ueber die Entsendung von Ukrainern aus Galizien und der Bukowina in die okkupierten Gebiete zwecks Organisierung und Verwaltung des ukrain. Schulwesens in diesen Gebieten," no date; "Denkschrift der Vereine a) der ukrainische paedagogische Verein in Lemberg; b) der ukrainische Mittelschullehrer-Verein 'Uchytelska Hromada' in Lemberg"; and "Grundriss der Geschichte des ukrainischen Schulwesens in Cholmland und Wolhynien," 4 February 1916, in Hornykiewicz, *Ereignisse*, I, pp. 109–118.
39. "Erlass Nr. 1302 des k. u. k. Min. d. Aeussern ueber die Regelung der Organisationsfrage des ukrain. Schulwesens im Cholmland sowie in jenen von oesterreichischen Truppen okkupierten russ. Gebieten Wolhyniens, deren dauernde Angliederung an Ostgalizien in Betrach kommen koennte," 23 March 1916; and "Ueber Stellungnahme des AOK zur Frage der Organisierung des ukrain. Schulwesens in den von den oesterreichischen Truppen okkupierten russ. Gebieten," 10 April 1916, in Hornykiewicz, *Ereignisse*, I, pp. 118–121.
40. "Gesuch die Herausgabe einer ukrain. Zeitung im besetzten russ. Gebiet betreffend," 7 October 1915; and the responses from the Foreign Ministry and AOK, dated 12 October 12 and 13 October 1915, in Hornykiewicz, *Ereignisse*, I, pp. 209–214.
41. See the documents, dated November 1915, in Hornykiewicz, *Ereignisse*, I, pp. 214–215.
42. "Koenigreich Ungarn und die ukrainische Frage," (October 1916; meeting with Tisza in December 1915), Zhuk collection, vol. 13, file 18; "Uebersetzung eines Briefes eines angesehenen Ukrainers aus Luck (Wolhynien)," 27 January 1916, in Hornykiewicz, *Ereignisse*, I, p. 216.
43. "Polish Declaration of Statehood and ULU," (November 1916), Zhuk collection, vol. 13, file 19. On 14 November 1916, and again on 5 February 1917, ULU sent official protests to the Foreign Minister, Count Czernin, on the Polish declaration and the incorporation of Ukrainian lands into the envisioned Polish state. See vol. 13, file 21; and Hornykiewicz, *Ereignisse*, I, pp. 221–222.
44. "Die Stellungnahme der Kriegsgefangenen Ukrainer zur Angelegenheit des selbststaendigen Polen," Zhuk collection, vol. 13, file 20. The questionnaire and summary report were signed by M. Saevych, *chetar'* of the Ukrainian Sich Sharpshooters and "decorated (*zasl.*) organizer" of Ukrainian schools in Volynia before the war. The resolution was based on a discussion of the responses to the questionnaires.

CHAPTER 4

The Brusilov Offensive and the Second Russian Occupation Regime

IN JUNE 1916 THE RUSSIAN ARMY LAUNCHED A SUCCESSFUL ATTACK against the Central Powers in what has become known as the Brusilov offensive, in honor of the commander-in-chief of the Southwestern Front. The offensive regained Bukovyna and a large part of eastern Galicia (Stanislav, Kolomyia, L'vov, and Tarnopol) for Russia.[1] In their increasing disenchantment with the Central Powers' support for their strivings and with the launching of the Brusilov offensive in June 1916, Ukrainian politicians made new appeals to Russian elites for a more liberal solution of the Ukrainian problem within the confines of Russia. The Ukrainian Bureau operating from Lausanne asked for guarantees that Ukrainians would not be persecuted. Foreign Minister Sazonov, soon to be dismissed from his position in a conservative coup in the Council of Ministers, advised Alekseev to make some reassuring proclamations that repressive measures would not be taken against Ukrainians in Galicia as long as those Ukrainians comported themselves as loyal citizens. But those guilty of crimes, of course, would face prosecution according to the law.[2]

Shortly after the invasion, the Ukrainian Committee, a body speaking for both ULU and the General Ukrainian National Committee, condemned the new occupation authorities for repeating all the mistakes of the first occupation regime and thereby reinforcing the worst possible conclusion about Russia, namely, that it really was engaged in a life and death struggle with the Ukrainian movement. The Committee appealed to all the peoples of the civilized world to support the Ukrainian people's right to national self-determination and national self-defense. Ukraine, in their stirring proclamation, faced a future of trenches, grenades, blood, homelessness, and the material ruination of its land.[3]

Still, the second Russian occupation of Galicia showed some signs of moderation and that the military authorities had learned some lessons from what they perceived to have been mistakes. After the first Russian occupation regime was forced to evacuate with the retreating armies, Governor-General Bobrinskii's staff was relocated to Kiev and instructed to conduct a study of the errors of the first occupation administration to avoid repeating them again during the expected second time round and to thereby "restore the prestige of Russian power in the broadest sense." Bobrinskii's commission concluded that the main source of the administration's difficulties was "the low educational and moral levels of the local officials" who had been reassigned to occupied Galicia. But it also acknowledged that it proceeded too quickly and brutally in reforming educational and cultural life there.[4] One commission member argued that the mistakes stemmed from a lack of unity in the administration of the territories and the contradictory war aims that were pursued by the Russian authorities; some of the occupation authorities were waging a war of national liberation while others viewed their efforts as a conquest. Bobrinskii himself criticized the nationalist agendas of various public organizations that had descended upon Galicia as interfering in the military's task of maintaining order in the occupied territory. The Kadet organ *Rech'* and the Kiev daily *Kievlianin* echoed these appeals for greater tolerance in policy toward language, religion, and cultural life.

Elsewhere in the Russian government, notably in the Special Political Department (*Osobyi politicheskii otdel*, or OPO) of the Foreign Ministry, a similar rethinking of occupation policy was undertaken. The Department, established in late 1916 originally as the Vatican-Slavic Department to reflect the anxieties about the western borderlands, was made up of several Russian diplomats who had been called back to Russia after the outbreak of war but who also maintained ties with "residents" (most likely, spies) in neutral capitals who kept track of German and Austrian policy toward several nationalities: (1) Poles and Carpatho-Rusyns; (2) Czechoslovaks, including Czech and Slovak prisoners-of-war in Russian camps; and (3) southern Slavs and Hungarians.[5] The Ukrainian experts included B. A. Budilovich, son of a well-known Slavic linguist and opponent of the Ukrainophiles Anton Budilovich; D. N. Vergun, former representative of St. Petersburg Telegraph Agency (and probably Russian intelligence) in Austria-Hungary, and A. Sobolevskii, chairman of the St. Petersburg Slavic Benevolent Society. They recommended new policies in the occupied territories in response to the Germans' encouragement of local languages during their recent occupation, in some cases even banning the use of Russian. The recommendations did not mean any abandonment of the Great Russian project of "reuniting" the three tribes (Russians, Little Russians, and Belarusans) in one state led by Russia, but they concluded that "positive" measures of encouraging the Russian language and culture worked better than repressive ones, such as banning the Ukrainian language and shutting down all Ukrainian-language publications and institutions.

Typical of this change in orientation was a memorandum prepared by Aleksei Gerovskii, who continued to believe that "Ukrainian separatism, which was directed at the weakening and dismembering of Russia, is one of the most serious issues in Russian domestic politics. One of the major results of the current war ought to be an end to Ukrainian irredenta. A successful liquidation of the Ukrainian question in Galicia would in part render less harmful the "Ukrainians" in Russia, who have become accustomed to view in Galicia a sort of Piedmont." He also warned that Bukovyna also posed a risk of the "Mazepist" movement similar to the role that the Cracow republic played after the partitions of Poland. Characteristically, Gerovskii never refers to Ukrainians without quotation marks and speaks of the local "Russian dialect"; still, he warns against creating "needless martyrs for the Ukrainian idea." He not only advised against closing the Ukrainian press, assuming, however, that once it was cut off from foreign (Austrian) financial sources it would close of its own inertia, but also against closing private Ukrainian schools, on the same assumption that they would wither for lack of financing. In particularly bitter remarks, he observed that "Ukrainian schools with their corrupted Little Russian language of instruction were, for Russian Galicians, as much of a surrogate for real Russian schools as the Union was a surrogate for Orthodoxy." Another recommendation that would appear frequently in both Russian and German analyses of the Ukrainian question was agrarian reform, in order to undercut the Ukrainian nationalists' appeals to the peasantry. Not surprisingly, Gerovskii was prepared to sacrifice Polish landowners, whose loyalty he declared Russian authorities could not count on in any event, Jewish business owners whom he hated with particular force, and the principle of private property. He insisted that Russia had to demonstrate to the Galician-Russian peasantry that it would liberate it not only "in the political, but in the economic and social senses too." As they had with many such recommendations, his superiors rejected this radical set of proposals. Gerovskii also recommended change in religious politics and "to support the point of view of Galician Uniates that the Union and Orthodoxy were one and the same. This translated into dropping the demand that believers formally convert from Uniate to Orthodox faith, but also for sending to Galicia educated priests who would be closer to their Uniate counterparts, among whom higher education was the norm.[6]

Another expert whose recommendations reflected the urgency of a new orientation for Russia in occupied Galicia was V. P. Svatkovskii, a journalist and spy operating out of Bern who reported back to Petrograd on German and Austrian politics and policies. He realized that his recommendations were radical and insisted to his reader that he "was absolutely opposed to the political and nationalist-separatist ideals of the Ukrainian movement" and considered it a great sin against Russia. The national and cultural demands of the Ukrainian programs were, in his opinion, excessive and harmful. Still, this basic viewpoint ought not to excuse "the sad fact of the complete absence of tact and tactics that are necessary to deal with the Ukrainian question in our favor." Parting ways with Gerovskii, however, who believed that the Ukrainian movement was weak and without any serious social support and would wither away on its own, Svatkovskii argued that the Ukrainian movement was a serious force to be reckoned with. Whereas Gerovskii and others had interpreted the absence of any Ukrainian separatist activism during the first Russian occupation as evidence of the Ukrainians' weakness, Svatkovskii offered an alternative analysis based on the local "Russian" population's Polonophobia. The Russian occupation was viewed by many as a liberation from Polish domination. And whereas the Russophobia and hatred of the "Moskaly" existed more in theory than practice, the Polonophobia was based on very real property relations and political and social hierarchies that excluded or marginalized Ukrainians in eastern Galicia. Svatkovskii criticized Bishop Evlogii by name for turning Ukrainians against Russia with his policies of persecution of the Greek Catholic Church.

Svatkovskii, from his vantage point in neutral Switzerland, had a keen sense of the geopolitical shifts in the first two years of war. The problem of Galicia, which had only recently been a delicate balance of the interests of Vienna, the Vatican, and the Poles, now had a new player, the Germans, who felt few of the constraints that their Habsburg allies had evolved over decades of rule in the region. In addition, Svatkovskii observed that the Hungarians were pursuing an ever more independent policy and appeared to have in mind an annexation of Galicia to Hungarian lands with autonomy similar to that of Croatia. In these new and fraught conditions, Svatkovskii argued that Russia could give Ukrainians that which Hungarians could not, namely "the immediate unification of all Ukraine, all 35 millions of the Little Russian or Ukrainian population." But now, Russia should offer something, even if only symbolic, to indicate its aims in the region. The promise of unifying Ukraine would be so attractive to Ukrainian activists, he speculated, that they would be happy even with small concessions at this point. He produced evidence for such a positive reorientation on the part of Ukrainian activists from the local Ukrainian émigré community in Switzerland.[7]

In a remarkable exchange of documents, Mikhail Tyshkevich, a prominent landowner from Kyiv guberniia, had already sent a very loyal telegram to the tsar in the name of Ukrainians by late summer 1915. The tsar answered via a telegram drafted by his court minister, Count Frederiks (in French), "His majesty has commanded me to thank you, and also the group of Ukrainians gathered in Switzerland, for the feelings expressed in your telegram." This was the first time that the word *Ukrainians*, as opposed to Little Russians, was ever uttered by the tsar. Svatkovskii made contact with Tyshkevich and relayed some of his proposals to his superiors in Petrograd. Tyshkevich, not surprisingly holding the views of a major landowner, gave preference to the national over the social factors in Ukraine, and did not encourage any radical land reform. He felt concessions on the "national" issue would diminish the pernicious influence of socialist propaganda among the peasants. Among these recommendations was one for a proclamation by the tsar that his son, the tsarevich, would be Hetman of Little Russia, and for the printing of portraits of the tsarevich Aleksei in Ukrainian costume.[8] Tyshkevich went on to recommend that Russia publish an official newspaper in Ukrainian in Kiev, "which would strictly defend the unity of the empire, but also serve as an indicator of the readiness of the government to meet the cultural desires of a certain part of the population." Finally, Svatkovskii passed along a recommendation that the Russian government make contact with Ukrainian leaders in Russia and Austria, with the exception of those openly hostile to Russia like Levytsky and Vasylko, the Austrian parliamentary deputies: "With minimal expression of good will from Russia it will be possible to deal a general blow to the Austrian orientation of the Ukrainian movement with great chances for success."

Finally, Svatkovskii reported that the Austrians too were learning lessons from their past mistakes. For the first time since the 1870s, they had appointed as viceroy a non-Pole, General German Kolar, who immediately upon arrival instructed his officials to respect the use of the Ukrainian language in official institutions. Shortly after the restoration of Austrian rule, Wilhelm Habsburg, the successor to the Habsburg throne, made a tour of Galicia and addressed "his" subjects in the Ukrainian language. Ukrainians were being actively recruited into the officer corps of the royal and imperial army. And, most alarming to Svatkovskii, was the news of special Austrian and German prisoner-of-war camps for Ukrainians that were privileged materially in comparison with the general camps for Russian POWs. Recently the ULU had gained permission from the German and Austrian High Commands to conduct agitational work among the prisoners in Ukrainian language, literature, and history. The camps also published their own newspapers in Ukrainian.[9] M. Bibikov, who had visited the camps in Rastatt and Salzwedel, reported that the propaganda efforts "were on a solid base and had very satisfying results." The camp authorities had authorized 40,000 of these prisoners to form units of a future Ukrainian army; they performed their drills in Ukrainian uniform.[10]

In a November 1916 memorandum Svatkovskii again urged Russian officials to bring together all moderate and reasonable Ukrainian forces who were united on a platform of "autonomy of Ukraine as part of Russia." He even included Ukrainian socialists from the *Borotba* faction as "decent people." He warned that the Germans were already supporting "their" Ukrainians with the aim of including Ukraine in a German plan of Mitteleuropa as outlined in the writing of Friedrich Naumann.[11] He attached another letter from Tyshkevich, in which the Ukrainian proposed even more serious concessions to the Ukrainian movement, including a Ukrainian university, the encouragement, and not merely toleration, of Ukrainian schools, equalization of the rights of Ukrainian and Russian languages, all the while "strictly punishing any manifestations of separatism" under the slogan "punish Mazepa but don't persecute Khmelnytsky." Furthermore, he demanded that the Russian government free the hundreds and thousands of representatives of the Galician intelligentsia deported to the interior of Russia, open the press and all societies, and, once again, send the tsarevich on a symbolic goodwill trip to L'vov. Svatkovskii expressed his own disagreement with several of these recommendations, but might also have been hiding some of his own more radical proposals behind Tyshkevich's name.[12] In any event, many of these recommendations would finally be adopted only after the fall of the Romanovs and the formation of the Provisional Government in revolutionary Petrograd.

The new occupation document that emerged reflected some of these conclusions. Indeed, the rhetoric of the second invasion and occupation regime no longer contained the grandiose claims of unification and reunification of Rus. The Russian language would still serve as the official government language, but the governor-general could also permit the use of local languages if recognized as necessary. This was meant to include Polish and Ukrainian languages. The Foreign Ministry also registered its concerns about the Ukrainian and Jewish questions, but came to contradictory recommendations on these matters. They urged that no more coercive measures be taken against the Jewish population, especially deportations and the taking of hostages, but insisted that there be no letting up in the struggle against "Ukrainophilism."

Emperor Nicholas, Chief of Staff Alekseev, and Brusilov wanted a new governor-general to implement the new regime, so Brusilov rejected the candidacy of Georgii Bobrinskii. But he also wanted a governor-general who at once had more authority from Petrograd to decide issues on his own and was more clearly subordinate to the Southwest Front's commander, namely, himself. The Foreign Ministry's Ukraine expert, V. Olferev, disagreed with Brusilov's ideas and argued for more demilitarization of the occupation regime and more coordination with civilian bureaucrats in the capital. The choice came down to two candidates, Aleksandr Krivoshein, until recently Ministry of Agriculture but out of favor with the conservative cabinet of Boris Shtiurmer, and S. D. Evreinov from the Army. Alekseev rejected Krivoshein's candidacy on the grounds that the occupation regime needed to be headed by a man with military experience. Evreinov, for his part, had already criticized some of the local excesses of the prior regime and was therefore viewed as unstatesmanlike. In the end, Brusilov got the candidate he wanted, General Fedor F. Trepov, despite the low opinion some held of him for his chaotic evacuation of the wounded from Kholm. Above all, Brusilov insisted on a military administration free of religious politics and all manifestations of nationalism. This also meant no radical reform measures in local life and more sensitivity to the cultural specificities of the local population. Trepov set up headquarters first in Tarnopol, and then in Chernovets.[13]

But the Russian authorities had not prepared themselves for the devastation that greeted them and that was the result of their own army's scorched-earth policy the year before, as well as the new destruction with the Austrian retreat and Russian advances. A Foreign Ministry official attached to Stavka reported back to the capital that "no trace remained of the former Galicia (of the first occupation)" and that the mood of the population was decidedly hostile to the Russians and sympathetic to the Austrians.[14] The 1915 harvest had perished, threatening epidemics during the winter. In these conditions, the new governor-general of Galicia proceeded to organize education, courts, and food supply in the occupied territories.

But when Trepov allowed schools to open with Polish and Ukrainian as their languages of instruction (though not Hebrew or German), the Foreign Ministry and Council of Ministers under the conservative Boris Shtiurmer protested that the Russian language ought to be introduced as quickly as possible. Shtiurmer warned that any weakening on the front of struggle with the Ukrainian movement would dangerously raise the hopes of the inhabitants of Russia's own Little Russian provinces and have "political consequences." Shtiurmer and the Foreign Ministry still adhered firmly to the policy of "reunification of Carpathian Rus" with the Russian State, as did a good part of Russian public opinion, but this time around the military authorities generally ignored these irredentist messages.[15]

February 1917: The Opposition Takes Over the War and Occupation Regime: Revolutionary Russia and New Ukrainian Piedmont

In February 1917 Emperor Nicholas II was persuaded to abdicate the throne, and shortly thereafter the Romanov dynasty came to an end in Russia. In its place arose a new set of authorities from the wartime opposition and public organizations, the Provisional Government and the Petrograd Soviet. In short order, the new regime was replicated in provincial capitals as well. In Kiev/Kyiv, the Executive Committee of the Council of Public Organizations (IKSOO in Russian abbreviation, ECCPO in English) and the Kiev Soviet of Workers' Deputies was joined, however, by the Central Rada, made up of moderate-left Ukrainian activists and rapidly emerging as a rival to Petrograd and its local agents, including in matters of occupation policy. The Provisional Government, made up of representatives of liberal and conservative public figures, quickly proclaimed itself in favor of continuing the war with the Central Powers in the name of "revolutionary Russia." Even the Provisional Government's reluctant partner, the Petrograd Soviet, dominated by the socialists of the Menshevik and Social Revolutionary parties, signed on to the war but insisted on the urgency of peace talks and that any postwar settlement reject annexations of new territories and populations without democratic referendums. The new authorities abolished discriminatory laws regarding nationality and religious confession, hoping thereby to satisfy most non-Russian political movements in the empire.[16] They were also pressured into adopting major reforms in the Russian Army that aimed at its democratization, but quickly led to its politicization along several lines. Now that the war had gone on for far longer than any of its launchers had anticipated, with far greater costs to the populations and economies of Europe, including and especially Russian Europe, all these factors contributed to a reshaping of the politics of war and occupation.

The agents of the Special Political Department continued to promote a new Ukrainian policy and appear to have been behind the organization of a meeting in May 1917 in Petrograd of "Russian refugees from Galician, Bukovynan, Ugorskaia [Transcarpathian] Rus." The meeting passed a resolution declaring its "desire to see Galician, Bukovynan, and Transcarpathian Rus united with a democratic Russian Republic" and thereby changed the terms of the debate from annexation to self-determination.

> The assembly was deeply certain that the unification of the aforementioned provinces would be but the restoration by a revolutionary Russian people of justice and of its duty to the Little Russian nationality which has over the course of centuries taken the most active role in the creation and strengthening of general Russian culture, and, like the Polish nation, has been divided by the senseless whim of autocratic tsars and Kaisers. (Miller, *Imperiia Romanovykh*, p. 184)

The report on this meeting was transmitted from Prime Minister L'vov's office to the Foreign Minister, Pavel Miliukov.[17] Among the several interesting aspects in this proposal were the replacement of Orthodox unity with revolutionary Slavic brotherhood, and the reference to Poland's partitions as part of a "democratic" national critique of autocracy and the Old Regime's imperial ways, more broadly replacing any formerly obligatory statements of loyalty to the tsar and the Romanov dynasty. Moreover, the unification that was stressed here was that of the Little Russian people rather than the former all-Russian idea, however much that was still operating in the minds of the protagonists.

The refugees from the Austrian lands formed one lobby group, but Russian Ukrainian activists who built their efforts around the Central Rada in Kyiv, and who also had their "representation" in Petrograd in the Ukrainian national committee there, soon rivaled them. Even earlier than the refugees' appeals, this group had paid a visit to the new government of Prince L'vov with a series of reforms in relations between Petrograd and the Ukrainian lands, among which were: appointing Ukrainians to key governing positions in Ukraine, including the occupied territories of Galicia and

Bukovyna; creating a commissar for Ukrainian affairs in the Petrograd government; the release of Galician and Bukovinian Ukrainians in Russian camps; and the satisfaction of cultural and educational needs.[18] The vague slogan of national-territorial autonomy began to take shape in these appeals from the Rada politicians to Petrograd, but soon they began to appeal to the international community of nations both within and without the Russian Empire.

The Provisional Government was initially more sympathetic to appeals from the non-Russians, but over time began to try to rein in the forces of national reform in the borderlands with the argument that the planned Constituent Assembly was the only appropriate body for deciding such far-reaching reforms. In early March the government resolved to "liberate immediately from detention the Metropolitan of Galicia, Count Sheptits'kyi," and to form a special commission in the Ministry of Justice to investigate the reasons for expelling Galician subjects [sic] in Russia."[19] The cause of Galician deportees had been one claimed by the liberal and socialist opposition, but also one that had garnered international condemnation of the old regime authorities. Another longtime demand of the Ukrainian movement was finally satisfied with the appointment of a Ukrainian activist, in this case Dmytro Doroshenko, as the regional commissar (with powers of general-governor) for occupied Galicia and Bukovyna. Doroshenko was a veteran of the Revolutionary Ukrainian Party and the Society of Progressists, had served as the representative of the Union of Cities for the Southwest Front on the occupied territories before 1917, and was one of the founders of the Central Rada. All these measures, including the authorization of the use of the Ukrainian language in teaching in schools in the Kiev/Kyiv school district, seemed to bode well for relations between the new authorities and Kiev/Kyiv.

Even these decisions, however, were not reached without considerable political fighting, above all on the appointment of Doroshenko as viceroy of occupied Galicia and Bukovyna. In late April, Doroshenko reported to the Rada on the strong opposition to naming a Ukrainian to this post among more nationalist Kadets like Paul Miliukov, the Foreign Minister, but also among the military, especially General Aleksei Brusilov, at the time commander of the Southwest Front but about to be promoted to comman-der-in-chief. Brusilov sent a representative to the meeting and a telegram conveying the urgency of appointing a civilian authority because "anarchy has broken out, the police have been dismissed, and there are no forces of local order." Still, a majority of the ministers of the Provisional Government, after swallowing their objections to the appointment of a Ukrainian, next debated on what powers to delegate to him. Here a split emerged over the relative power of the military and civilian spheres, with Miliukov arguing with Doroshenko that he should have the right to appeal to the government in Petrograd and merely had to inform Brusilov, the military authority. Much work was to be done with the civilian population and the reconstruction of the demolished economy of the region. In opposition, Alexander Guchkov, the Octobrist Minister of the Army, insisted that the needs of the army were paramount and that Doroshenko ought to be strictly subordinate to Brusilov and to the military's direction. The government did not resolve this issue, and Doroshenko would soon feel the consequences of the poorly defined nature of his powers. He did manage to persuade the Provisional Government coalition to appoint three more governors for the occupied territories from among the ranks of Ukrainian activists: Andrii Viazlov was appointed to Volynia, Oleksandr Lotots'kyi to Chernivtsi, and Ivan Kraskovs'kyi to Ternopil.[20] This team of Ukrainophile governors pursued a policy of Ukrainianization in the regional governmental apparatus, and during the months of May and June replaced all lower-level commissars with new officials who could claim revolutionary credentials.

One of the other matters discussed in Doroshenko's first report to the Rada as viceroy of occupied Austrian Ukraine was how to handle the now liberated Metropolitan Sheptits'kyi, who had asked in Petrograd for permission to return to Galicia. This had been denied on the grounds that it was not quite appropriate for an Austrian subject to be making his way through the rear of Brusilov's army. Instead, he was allowed to return to his brother in Podilia, but by way of Kiev/Kyiv. The Rada debated how to receive this hero, and now martyr, of the Galician national movement, especially in light of his apparently "new orientation" of working to avoid the incorporation of Galicia in a restored Poland. Sheptits'kyi's circle of Galician priests wanted to mount a great welcoming manifestation, but Doroshenko was worried about the political and religious consequences, since all these elements had "not forgotten about the Union and wanted to spread it now to Ukraine." In the end, it was decided to welcome him at a modest level (*ne zanadto pyshno*) and to present him as someone who had been a victim of the Old Regime. Even Hrushevs'kyi warned that the "black hundreds" forces of radical Russian nationalism were waiting for an opportunity to paint the Ukrainian movement as part of Sheptits'kyi's Catholicizing mission.[21]

Soon, however, under increasing pressures from returning radical exiles and in the face of rising disorder throughout the former Russian Empire, the national movement in Ukraine began to make further demands, starting with a statement from Petrograd in support of the autonomy of Ukraine in the name of a democratic federalist reorganization of the Russian state. In short order, the Kyiv-based national movement insisted on the right to send a representative to any postwar negotiations on the redrawing of borders, and that any such frontiers "be established in accordance with the will of the borderland populations." They also appealed to Poles and other non-Russian minorities in the empire who were striving for greater rights; and they raised concern about Ukrainians outside the ethnically most concentrated provinces in Left- and Right-Bank Ukraine.[22] All these developments in Petrograd and Kiev/Kyiv reinforced a more Ukrainophile occupation regime in Galicia and Bukovyna, with Russian Ukraine now able to play the role of Ukrainian Piedmont instead of Austrian Ukraine, whose role had been suspended by the first Russian occupation.

The Ukrainianization of the cultural and educational life as well as the administrative personnel of the region soon provoked negative reactions within the military and "civilian" forces. The tensions between Doroshenko's efforts at reconstructing the devastated region and reassuring the civilian population that its rights would not be violated again so brutally and the military's priorities came to the fore during the failed June offensive, launched by Kerensky, now War Minister and Prime Minister, partly in hopes of restoring the morale and combat-readiness of the Russian Army. The Austrians counterattacked in the "Ternopil' breakthrough" and temporarily retook most of Galicia during the late summer, but the Russians took back most of what they lost. Indeed, Doroshenko's administration was suspended for two months, while the Russians regained control of the region. He insisted that his team had operated according to the principle that "as long as it didn't harm the interests of the army, one had to alleviate the condition of the local population, revive urban self-government, courts, and schools and to conduct this policy in a spirit of religious and national tolerance." This proved nearly impossible to realize in the conditions of the front-line army's overwhelming presence in the area and the urgency of keeping that army fed and otherwise outfitted. The burden for this provisioning fell almost entirely on the local population who were subjected to forced labor and carting obligations, as well as providing food and other supplies, especially horses and oxen, that they themselves desperately needed after nearly three years of constant ruination. Doroshenko reported that children and women were reinforcing teams to repair roads and other reconstruction projects and that the population was "in the position of slaves" in the reconquered provinces. The requisitions effort was headed up by the local representative of the Ministry of Agriculture, one Grigorenko, who had recruited as assistants right-bank agrarians, mostly from the landowner class and who thereby avoided military service. Doroshenko saw this as the explanation why the requisition burden fell so unevenly and unfairly on the peasants; large landowners and priests were exempt. The officials' goals were to seize as much as they could, with no apparent sympathy for the local population. Corruption and bribe-taking were rampant.

Although these wartime hardships were not motivated by any particular ill will on the part of the military to the inhabitants of the occupied territories, nonetheless, according to Doroshenko, military discipline had sunk so low that soldiers were reported to be engaging in all sorts of wanton brutality, from rapes and general pillage to murder. They had the attitude that since they had fought to hold these territories, everything "was ours: you and everything you have." Atrocities were particularly common among members of the "Wild Division," who were spurred on by General Lavr Kornilov, recently promoted to commander-in-chief of the Russian Army. Special targets were local Jews; in Brody, murders and vandalism had become an everyday phenomenon. Appeals were made to the military authorities and to the army committees, who released some appeals of their own, but to little avail. Doroshenko further lamented that any efforts to revive education or justice in the region were stymied by the army's occupation of all available buildings. He concluded with sad irony that in this era of great freedom, the Galician population knew nothing of these new gains. With one hand, he was issuing proclamations about the new freedoms, while with the other he was signing orders for labor and other obligations.

All attempts to appeal to the military authorities were met with the standard reply that war was war and the army's needs were the highest priority for the local administration. But he also faced accusations of "Austrophilism" for his efforts to defend the local population. He and several others on his team were convinced that the headquarters of the various armies, and particularly their counterintelligence officers, were not just resentful adherents of the Old Regime, but were also under the sway of the "Moscophiles," including several who had had clashes with the prior occupation administration and were embittered on that account as well.

As he had elsewhere in the revolutionary movement, he suspected that dismissed police officials, who were linked to the Black Hundreds movement, were finding places in the military apparatus. An expectation of some action by the "forces of counterrevolution" was in the air across the country, and the Kornilov putsch attempt against the Provisional Government in a few weeks was an indication that those who raised the alarm were not wrong in their analysis. Doroshenko reported several arrests of Ukrainian officials by military authorities on "evidence" provided by counterintelligence. When higher military authorities investigated several of these charges, most were dismissed as having no basis. This reactionary politics also shaped the brutal behavior of Russian troops during their recent retreat from the Germans. Pogroms were conducted by members of the "Wild Division" in Kalush against Jews and Ukrainians, and also in Stanislavov and Ternopil'. One final catastrophe that Doroshenko tried to halt was the army's order to evacuate all males aged 18 to 43, together with their household and horses. Of course, the army could barely evacuate its own forces, let alone the bulk of the civilian population, but neither Kornilov, the commander-in-chief, nor his commissar, Savenkov, would relent on this brutal measure which, not surprisingly, created a new wave of refugees that the authorities further in the interior were incapable of accommodating. One of the conclusions drawn in the Central Rada ranks was that the war itself was creating intolerable conditions and that a peace treaty had to be pursued immediately.[23]

NOTES

1. For more on the Brusilov offensive, see Norman Stone, *The Eastern Front*, chapter 11; see also A. A. Brusilov, *Moi vospominaniia* (Moscow: Rosspen, 2001), pp. 161–196.
2. Bakhturina, *Politika Rossiiskoi Imperii*, pp. 211–212.
3. "Aufruf der Ukrainischen Komitees an die Voelker der Kulturwelt ueber die Unterdrueckungs- und Verfolgungsmethoden des ukrain. Nationalen Lebens in Russland und ueber die Freiheitsbestrebungen des ukrain. Volkes," 22 September 1916, in Hornykiewicz, *Ereignisse*, I, pp. 217–221.
4. See Bakhturina, *Politika Rossiiskoi Imperii*, pp. 214–224. The results of the commission's findings were summarized in "Otchet kantseliarii voennogo general-gubernatora Galitsii" (Kiev, 1916), cited earlier in the chapter on the first Russian occupation regime.
5. The history of the Political Department is found in a new book by Alexei Miller, *Imperiia Romanovykh i natsionalism* (Moscow: Novoe literaturnoe obozrenie, 2006), p. 173–189.
6. Miller, *Imperiia Romanovykh*, pp. 177–79. Gerovskii was the grandson of the well-known Russophile Adolf Dobrianskyi. Miller cites documents in the Archive of the Foreign Policy of the Russian Empire, f. 135.

7. Miller, *Imperiia Romanovykh*, pp. 180–189. Svatkovskii's first memo was dated 30 November 1915, "The Ukrainian Question on the Eve of the Spring Campaign"; he developed his ideas further over the course of 1916.

8. This copied the Austrians' grooming the successor to the throne, Wilhelm Habsburg, who took on the name Vasyl' Vyshyvanyi, as their candidate for Ukrainian Hetman. This prospect was dangled before Pavel Skoropadsky, who thought he was Hetman of Ukraine, during 1918.

9. On the activities of ULU in the camps, see the reports of Andry Zhuk in his archive, Zhuk Collection, MG 30, C 167, vol. 12.

10. Miller, *Imperiia Romanovykh*, pp. 185–186.

11. Ibid., 186–187. The Germans encouraged the Verein zur Unterstuetzung der Ukrainischen Freiheitsbestrebungen. In Vienna ULU published its *Vistnyk Soiuza vyzvolennia Ukrainy*.

12. Ibid., pp. 188–189.

13. The governor-generalcy was divided further into two provinces, Chernivtsi, whose governor was Ligin, and Ternopil,' whose governor was Ivan Chartorizhskii.

14. Cited in Bakhturina, *Politika Rossiiskoi Imperii*, p. 217.

15. Ibid., pp. 223–24.

16. Browder and Kerensky, I, pp. 211–212.

17. Miller, *Imperiia Romanovykh*, pp. 189–190.

18. The best brief account of the Petrograd government's dealing with the Ukrainian national movement during 1917 is Wolodymyr Stojko, "Ukrainian National Aspirations and the Russian Provisional Government," in Hunczak, *The Ukraine*, pp. 4–32. His account is based on the memoirs and participant histories of some of the key figures in the Kyiv-Petrograd relationship: I. G. Tsereteli, *Vospominaniia o fevral'skoi revoliutsii*, 2 vols. (Paris: Mouton & Co., 1963); D. Doroshenko, *Istoriia Ukrainy, 1917–1923 rr.*, Vol. I (2d ed.; New York: Bulava Publishing Corporation, 1954); O. Lotots'kyi, *Storinky mynuloho*, Vol. III (Warsaw: Ukrainskyi Naukovyi Instytut, 1934); V. Chernov, *The Great Russian Revolution* (New York: Russell and Russell, 1966); and V. Vynnychenko, *Vidrodzhennia natsii*, Vol. I (Kiev-Vienna: Vyd. Dzvin, 1920).

19. 8 March 1917, in Browder and Kerensky, II, p. 838.

20. See Doroshenko's report in "Protokoly zasidan' komitetu Tsentral'noi Rady," 26 April 1917, *Ukrains'ka Tsentral'na Rada: Dokumenty i materialy*, 2 vols. (Kyiv: Naukova Dumka, 1996), vol. I, pp. 75–77. Viazlov and Lotots'kyi were members of the Society of Progressists; Lotots'kyi also was prominent in the Radical Democratic Party, had chaired the Ukrainian National Council in Petrograd in March 1917. Viazlov and Kraskovs'kyi were veterans of the public organizations and had served in Galicia as representatives to the committee of the Southwest Front from the All-Russian Union of Cities.

21. *Ukrains'ka Tsentral'na Rada*, I, pp. 76–77.

22. See documents in Browder and Kerensky, I, pp. 370–372. On 21–28 September, 1917, Kiev/Kyiv welcomed representatives of the major imperial nationalities in a People's Congress that elected Hrushevs'kyi honorary president and tried to raise the pressure on Kerensky's quickly failing government in Petrograd.

23. Doroshenko, "Zasidannia komitetu Tsentral'noi Rady," 22 July 1917, *Ukrains'ka Tsentral'na Rada*, I, pp. 184–189.

CHAPTER 5
The German Occupation of Ukraine 1918

THE OCCUPATION OF UKRAINE IN 1918 by the coalition forces of Germany and Austria-Hungary was fraught with contradictions from the beginning.[1] The terms of the occupation were only partly worked out in the Brest Treaty,[2] which for the Central Rada government of Myhailo Hrushevs'kyi extended its life for another couple of months by displacing the Bolshevik regime in Kyiv/Kiev and compelling the new Soviet regime in Moscow to recognize, however reluctantly, the Ukrainian People's Republic. In January 1918 Bolshevik forces, led by Mikhail Murav'ev,[3] entered Ukraine from the northeast, shelled Kyiv/Kiev for eleven days, and then occupied the city for another two weeks before the German forces sent them fleeing back to Russia. Although the brief occupation did not leave any lasting changes, this first taste of Bolshevik rule was very alarming for the residents of the city. Not only was this their first taste of bombing campaigns, but also of violent civil war. Much damage occurred in the city's central districts, including the home of Myhailo Hrushevs'kyi. Ukrainian institutions were shut down and the Ukrainian language replaced by Russian. But the invaders did not spare Russians either, if they represented hostile institutions or classes. Metropolitan Vladimir of Kyiv was dragged from his residence and brutally murdered, as were approximately 2,500 Russian officers.[4]

The brief but traumatic experience with Bolshevik occupation made the arrival of the German troops and the return of the Rada government on 2 March 1918 seem something of a relief, though few inhabitants of the Ukrainian capital viewed the Germans as liberators. No one threw flowers at the arriving troops, as they would for the arrival of White Russian General Anton Denikin a little more than a year later. Kyiv/Kiev received the Germans with an air of quiet resignation. Locals respected German military strength and hoped to be saved from the Bolsheviks; indeed, German order, even if it was guaranteed by military occupation, was expected to be an improvement over the "communist dictatorship."[5] For the Central Powers, especially for the Austrians who were experiencing severe domestic food shortages, the treaty was greeted as the *Brotfrieden*, or bread peace. The official aims of the German occupation were "the restoration of the power of the Central Rada, the establishment of peace and order in the countryside and the beginning of trade relations." More specific aims included the seizure of the rail lines to Kiew.[6] But very quickly the occupying powers grew frustrated with the socialist nationalists of the Rada, now renamed the Ukrainian People's Republic, and found another solution to their problems of governance in a coup in late April that put in power Pavel Skoropadsky, a former general in the Russian Imperial Army, as Hetman of Ukraine.[7]

Several difficulties plagued the new occupation, starting with its emergence as almost an afterthought to the Brest negotiations, with little or no prior planning and no division of responsibilities between Austria-Hungary and Germany. Within weeks after arriving, General Groener sent anxious requests to his superiors for more troops, since Ukraine was several times the size of all of Germany.[8] The asymmetrical relationship, with a clearly dominant Germany frequently ignoring a weaker Austria-Hungary, was at the base of many tensions. The two putative allies had different interests in a whole range of areas, from the future of Poland to the general postwar settlement. For example, the Germans, despite wartime promises to help resurrect a Polish state, nonetheless feared the resurrection of a strong and expansionist Slavic neighbor on their border, as did most Ukrainian elites, whereas the "Austro-Polish solution" was bound to favor Poland over Ukraine in any postwar reconfiguration of borders and kingdoms. At various times, Austrian authorities promised Poles a special status of crownland equivalent to that of Hungary since 1867; furthermore, the Austrians were loath to promise the Ukrainians any change in status because of their historic reliance on the Poles to rule over the Ukrainian population in Galicia.[9] But in one desperate concession to the Ukrainians during the Brest negotiations, the Austrians promised a division of Galicia into its Polish and Ukrainian portions, with the annexation of Bukovyna to the Ukrainian portion. This was later repudiated and even denied by the Austrians, and added to the Ukrainians' sense of the Austrians as dishonest double-dealers.[10] Another postwar option discussed by the Austrians and viewed unfavorably by the Germans was the Hetman throne going to a member of the Habsburg house, in particular to Archprince Wilhelm.[11] The sensitivities of the then sitting hetman, Skoropadsky, were of little concern to the Austrians, and they had settled on this solution as a way of solving the problems of ethnic boundaries. In general, the Austrians did not take seriously the Holubovych government of the former Rada, whereas the Germans, at least initially, tried to avoid appearing to interfere too blatantly in Ukrainian affairs.[12]

On the larger question of the postwar world, the Austro-Hungarian elites were trying desperately to contain the newly unleashed forces of national secession and ethnic hostility in order to preserve what they could of their ever more fragile system of imperial compromises. They were thereby inclined to conservative solutions and minimal costs to their stability. The German Reich, on the other hand, under its aggressive emperor, was hell-bent on expanding German power in the world, even at the expense of existing empires and nations. The violent detachment of the *Randvoelker* from the Russian Empire, which had been pursued since the beginning of the war, now became a cardinal feature of German policy and involved the Germans in military occupations and diplomatic intrigues that alarmed their Austrian partners. In a particularly revealing note from Chief of the Austrian General Staff Arthur Arz to Foreign Minister Stefan Burian, Arz complained that Austria really had no clear war aims as late as the summer of 1918, whereas the Germans viewed Ukraine as "the surest way to Mesopotamia, Arabia, Baku and Persia." Germany had designs on the Donbass, despite its being formally assigned to the Austrian sphere, and also planned to remove Odessa from Austria's jurisdiction. He concluded that "we have only ourselves to blame" because of our "inner weaknesses," that the Austrians were helpless to stop the Germans from pursuing their goals, and had best work with them hand in hand to extract what few benefits they could from the relationship.[13] Still, at one point when relations were at their worst, the Austrians demanded the resignation of Field Marshall Ludendorf if Austria-Hungary were to continue its alliance with Germany.[14]

Despite formal agreements dividing spheres of interest along geographic lines, the two occupiers nonetheless found themselves sharing jurisdiction over Kiew and agreeing to several districts where there would be mixed troop occupation. Because the lands of historic German colonists fell under the sphere of Austria-Hungary, the agreement stipulated that German-language troops be assigned to this area to avoid antagonizing a potentially loyal community.[15] The mutual hostility of the two occupying powers was also fed by suspicions that the other side was secretly trying to negotiate better conditions for itself with the local powers. The Austrians' relatively more desperate food situation at home inclined them to seek more autonomy from the joint German-Austrian grain collection stations.[16] They appointed a commander-in-chief of Ostarmee, General Alfred Kraus, to coordinate activities with "unlimited power" from the strategic Black Sea port of Odessa; Krauss became the Austrians' consul in Ukraine.[17]

The Austrians' commandant in Odessa, Field Marshal von Boeltz, appeared to cooperate with the Ukrainian commissar for Odessa to negotiate on behalf of the "Austrian" provinces; this effort provoked protests from the Germans who insisted on a unified command of the country and resisted its regionalization. The Germans made blatant appeals to the Ukrainian government in this vein and argued, somewhat disingenuously, that they were defending the integrity of the Ukrainian territories.[18]

Both occupying powers engaged in a perpetual effort to win the favor of those local political and social forces they thought might be useful now and in the future. The Germans tended to be influenced most by the Ukrainian national parties,[19] whereas the Austrians, located primarily in the south, made contact with local Russian monarchist and nationalist organizations.[20] Both of these sets of local organizations in turn sought favor with the occupying powers and tried to play them off one another while seeking their own advantage against the Hetman government. It was rare that Austria-Hungary and Germany agreed on fundamental issues of the occupation in Ukraine; more often, they were operating at cross-purposes and bringing closer the ultimate downfall of the occupation regime. The Rada, for example, made demands on the Germans that they push further to occupy Odessa themselves (and thereby shut out the Austrians, whom they mistrusted and accused of pillage) and to seize Kharkiv and the Donets Basin as well.[21]

Of course, the persistent differences between the two allies were far from being the most serious problem facing the occupation. Above all, the invading forces encountered devastation and widespread discontent among the population. The German invaders faced fierce resistance from workers' Red Guards units and front-line soldiers in the urban areas, but also from peasants as they tried to establish their control in the countryside. The conquest of Ukraine lasted nearly two months. Within weeks the occupation authorities were resorting to extreme measures of repression; for every German or Polish soldier killed or wounded, local military authorities were to shoot the first ten "Russian" soldiers or inhabitants that were seized. The death sentence was ordered for any disruption of the food supply or violation of other state property.[22] Military censorship was introduced for all newspapers, and the first newspaper was closed for anti-German agitation. According to S. Sumskii, who worked at *Kievskaia mysl'*, the Germans were particularly offended by an article in *Borot'ba*, a newspaper identified with the current prime minister, Holubovych, in which the author warned that the Germans risked antagonizing the peasantry with their behavior as conquerors. The "moderate and careful article" suggested that the German high command rein in some of their unruly units to preserve "friendly relations between sovereign Ukraine and Germany." The newspaper remained closed for a few days, and then reopened with a promise not to print articles critical of the Germans.[23] The German commander seized the building of the Kiew/Kyiv nobility on Duma Square, and German troops began outfitting the city with telegraph and telephone poles; local inhabitants perceived the wiring they encountered everywhere they walked as the material symbol of their shackling by the new authorities. All this was done in the cause of "creating order" (*Wir werden Ordnung schaffen*), as German soldiers and officers explained their mission to local inhabitants.[24]

Before long the occupation forces reached the considerable number of 300,000, but the commanders of both coalition armies, the Germans and Austria-Hungary, constantly appealed to their superiors to add to those numbers. German General Wilhelm Groener complained that the invasion had been undertaken without much forethought or planning. He recalled that it was originally thought that the occupation forces could preserve order by holding only one-third of the country; but without the strategic energy resources of the Donbass, the capital was unable to function.[25] It quickly became clear that in allowing the Central Rada to continue to rule the country, the grain promised in the Brest Treaty would never be forthcoming; moreover, any efforts to collect the grain from the rural population added to the fires of peasant insurgency and rendered the military's hold over the land ever more tenuous.[26]

Still, the original intentions of the occupiers were to leave the Ukrainian government in place, while hoping that its leftist policies, particularly in the agrarian realm, would be moderated. The Rada, however, confounded all its critics by proclaiming its steadfast adherence to its previous policies, above all the nationalization of the land and the abolition of private property without compensation.[27] The most important dilemma that emerged for the occupiers, then, was the impotence of the Rada government in imposing order over the lands it claimed to govern and its ideological unwillingness to force the peasants to surrender their grain. The grain delivery provisions of the Brest Treaty were embarrassing to the Rada government and kept secret from the population.[28] The Germans also accused the Rada of refusing to acknowledge that the Ukrainian government had invited the Germans into their country. Before long, it became evident to local observers that the Germans were the real government of Ukraine, and they seemed only rarely to consult with their "allies." The Germans made their will known by posting signs in German and Russian with their latest decrees; Ukrainian government members often learned of these measures together with the local populace by reading the announcements.

By the end of March, however, both the diplomatic and military authorities in Kiew came to the conclusion that simple occupation—while allowing a nominally independent Ukrainian government to rule—could not be sustained; a consensus began to emerge that a more direct takeover of Ukraine by its occupiers would be necessary to ensure the effective exploitation of the desperately needed resources.[29] One proposal was to create a General-Gouvernement that was subordinated to the German Reich authorities. This was favored by the military, particularly General Groener, but the diplomats raised objections to any plan for a coup against the Social-Revolutionary-dominated Rada government. This would not play well at home, where social-democratic parties held powerful blocs in the *Reichstag*, nor with neutral foreign powers.[30] Moreover, the diplomats felt that a change in government might merely disrupt whatever grain and other deliveries were being made at a time when the survival of the Austrian state required 50,000 wagonloads of those supplies.[31] Instead, the occupiers sought means to moderate the "communistic" policies of the Rada ministers, in particular the abolition of private property. One idea was to invite German and Austrian Social-Democratic parliamentarians to meet with their Ukrainian counterparts.[32] In the meantime, Groener had finally won the removal of his superior, General Linsingen, and received welcome word of the appointment of Field Marshall von Eichhorn and of his own appointment as Eichhorn's chief of staff.[33]

The Rada's policies created considerable difficulties for German and Austrian authorities with Polish landowners, especially given Germany's promises to Polish elites to restore the nation after victory with generous borders. Polish landowners complained of anarchy and demanded that Ukrainian peasants be forced to reimburse landowners for any lands seized during the past years of revolutionary upheaval.[34] The Poles thereby added to the pressures facing the occupiers to take over more direct control of the country and replace or eliminate the current Ukrainian government.[35] Local non-Ukrainians observed that the one area where the German authorities gave the Ukrainian government power to act was in the "national" realm,

or "nationalistic" in the eyes of some. They perceived the Ukrainian nationalists as having decided to pursue a policy of Ukrainianization with no
holds barred, creating a hostile attitude toward everything perceived as
Russian, including arbitrary arrests of Jews suspected of being Bolshevik
collaborators. Irregular Ukrainian soldiers, who had taken the name
haidamaky and returned with the German invaders, established their headquarters at the Mikhailovskii monastery, where they interrogated, tortured,
and executed Jews. Jews were suspected of being spies and giving signals
to the Red Army during the recent invasion by Murav'ev. Before long the
Germans themselves demanded an end to these abuses.[36]

Finally, on 6 April, Field Marshal Eichhorn issued an order on seeding
the land in time for the planting season, which in effect began the campaign
to restore private property in the occupied territories,[37] leading to a violent
conflict with the Rada government, which protested the illegal intervention
in domestic affairs. Despite Ambassador Mumm's apparent personal
sympathies for the Ukrainian Prime Minister, Holubovych, he concluded
now that further negotiations would get the occupiers nowhere, and that
more drastic measures needed to be contemplated.[38]

The Occupiers Give Their Blessing to a Coup d'Etat

The Brest Treaty articles on grain deliveries were finally signed by both
sides on 23 April; that evening the military and diplomatic representatives
of the occupying states met and concluded that the Rada government
was an obstacle to maintaining peace in the land and guaranteeing the
desperately needed grain and other foodstuffs. Three days later Emperor
Wilhelm II wrote to Eichhorn with his approval of the candidacy of Pavel
Skoropadsky to replace the Rada government if the latter agreed to "our
conditions." Those conditions included: that no Ukrainian army shall
be formed, as long as Austro-Hungarian and German troops remain in
Ukraine; that occupation field courts try Ukrainians charged with crimes
against the occupiers; that all government offices and institutions be purged
of undesirable elements; and that all restrictions on private trade and
property be removed so as to restore the free circulation of goods and create
the conditions for the promised grain deliveries to the Central Powers.[39]
On 25 April, Eichhorn issued an order on military field courts, effectively
stripping Ukrainian judicial authorities of the right to try their own citizens.
The order read, "Irresponsible individuals and gangs are striving to terrorize

the population. Contrary to every law and to individual rights, they are arresting people in order to terrorize those who are prepared to cooperate with Germany to further the interests of their native land and the newly formed state."[40] The order further banned any assemblies that threatened the public order, as well as newspapers that agitated against social peace.

The matter of a coup against the Rada was now one of timing. The occupying authorities wanted to effect a change of government before the convening of the Ukrainian Constituent Assembly, scheduled for 12 May. In mid-April the Rada had provoked a confrontation with the German military authorities when it ordered the arrest of A. I. Dobryi, a Jewish director of the Kyiv/Kiew Bank who was working with the German forces. The Germans viewed this act as an arbitrary provocation and confronted the Holubovych government, demanding an explanation. In apparent retaliation, though subsequently repudiated by the German High Command, German officers began arresting members of the Central Rada ministries during one of their sessions. The indignant Ukrainian government demanded the immediate dismissal of Field Marshal Eichhorn.[41] The conflict between the Rada ministers and their erstwhile protectors played itself out against a backdrop of other political events that led to the proclamation of the Hetman state, namely a meeting of a "farmers'" movement.

The German military authorities clearly felt they had a government they could work better with in the Skoropadsky Hetman state, and they were willing to stand behind his regime from its inception. But they also harbored no illusions about the "fiction" of a completely independent, sovereign state. On the first days after the coup, General Groener and Ambassador Mumm met with leaders of the political parties to try—unsuccessfully, it turned out—to persuade them to work together with the new authorities. At the same time they tried not to be perceived as exerting too much pressure on the new government out of fear of giving ammunition to its enemies, who saw it as an illegitimate puppet of the Central Powers—especially after the unceremonious arrest by German officers of the Rada ministers while they convened, but also out of domestic German political sensitivities.[42] The Hetman reassured his German overlords with his proclamation of dictatorial powers and his lack of readiness to convene the Constituent Assembly or any other pre-parliamentary bodies until order had been restored to the Ukrainian land.[43] He also proceeded to overturn the Rada agrarian order—or disorder—by decreeing the restoration of private property in land and abolishing the notorious land committees. These measures met with the approval of the occupying authorities, who issued their own orders to his decrees. "The Germans were called by the Ukrainians to create order in the land," began one draft decree, and that order "will be achieved by force." Such was the introduction to an order banning strikes by railworkers and submitting the Ukrainian rail administration and its workers to German military law. The death penalty was introduced for any destruction of railroad property.[44]

But for all their improved relations with the new government, the occupying authorities made little progress in overcoming the major shortcoming of the prior government: its failure to gather grain for delivery to the Central Powers. This time, however, the Germans and their Austrian partners resolved to intervene more directly in introducing a network of grain centers, in Kyiv/Kiew and eight other provinces, that operated in parallel with analogous bodies of the new government.[45] The Germans insisted that Ukraine not export foodstuffs to any other state until it had met its obligations to the Central Powers and only after consulting with them. The Germans did not view this as an infringement on Ukrainian sovereignty, but as a rightful insistence on Ukraine's treaty obligations.[46] The Austrian delegates furthermore objected to permitting the Ukrainian cooperative movement any role in the grain collection and delivery process, since this would undermine the cartel-like arrangements that the occupiers hoped to set up.[47] And, as before, when peasants refused to cooperate peacefully with the grain authorities, they were frequently met with punitive battalions, some organized by local landlords eager to avenge their losses, but others as units of the occupying armies. This continuity in repressive policies sustained the widespread peasant opposition to the new regime in power.[48]

All these difficulties, however, did not discourage German capital from entertaining fantasies of wartime and especially postwar profits in Ukraine; very soon, representatives of major German firms began making research trips to the region and expected close cooperation and support from the local diplomatic and military authorities.[49] The German ambassador contrasted the recent, one-time extraction of resources in Belgium with a far longer-lasting set of economic relationships with Ukraine and urged that military means be replaced with more civilian methods of governance as soon as it proved feasible.[50] Meanwhile, the German Interior Ministry began to worry about Austrian competition in supplying airplanes to Turkey because of its [German] interest in assuring flyover rights for its planes in Poland and Ukraine and the use of Odessa as a stopover to Constantinople and the greater Middle East.[51]

Opposition to the New Regime: Insurgency and Terrorism

The socialist parties, which had formed the deposed Central Rada, began to mobilize almost immediately against the Hetman state, despite an initial offer from his government, under pressure from the Germans, to include their representatives. The parties refused to sanction the new state as legitimate and forbade its members from taking any positions with the dictatorship. This did not, however, prevent many of the former Rada officials from collaborating with the successor government; still, they served on their personal rights, not as representatives of the socialist parties. The Ukrainian socialist opposition agitated against the new regime and even sent numerous appeals to the German occupiers. Among the main charges made to the Germans was that the Hetman state was too Russian and failed to consolidate the progress made in Ukrainianizing public life under the previous government,[52] but they also objected to the continued use of punitive detachments, the restrictions on public assembly, and the censorship of the press.

The occupying authorities, particularly the Germans, found themselves in the curious position of receiving the political opposition and promising to persuade the Hetman of the wisdom of their position. The National Union forces insisted that they were the only "truly" Ukrainian party; any government that admitted Russians and Poles, especially in the considerable numbers now serving in the Hetman cabinet, could not consider itself Ukrainian. The Germans, frankly, were more interested in restoring the agricultural situation and sympathized with Skoropadsky when he argued that he sought out competent ministers above all, regardless of their national origin.[53] But the constant pressure and criticism from the opposition involved the Germans in endless conversations with the Hetman and his prime minister about changes in his cabinet to meet the "Ukrainian" complaints or in explaining to the opposition the logic of the Hetman's policies.[54]

The war of words was not as threatening as the use of violence, however. The terrorist traditions of several of the Russian and Ukrainian revolutionary parties, particularly the Socialist-Revolutionaries and anarchists, were revived and redirected against the Hetman government and its German and Austrian patrons. Skoropadsky's staff received constant reports of plots against his life, but he survived all such plans. The German commander-in-chief, Field Marshal Eichhorn, however, was not so lucky and was killed together with his adjutant by a bomb hurled at their car at the end of July 1918. The assassination of the German Ambassador in Moscow, Count Mirbach, coming fast on the murder of Eichhorn, sent ripples of anxiety through the German military and political elites, both in Kyiv/Kiew and Berlin.[55] The murders and plots for further attacks were part of a broad wave of revolutionary violence attributed to the left wing of the Socialist-Revolutionary party and its allies, who opposed the signing of the Brest treaty with the Central Powers as an act of betrayal of the Revolution.

Leftist opposition was not the only cause for anxiety among the new government and its international patrons. In particular, Russian monarchist and right-wing organizations, notably the Kiev National Center—a branch of the All-Russian National Center—and the Union for the Rebirth of Russia, viewed Ukraine as a launching pad for their recovery of Russia, "one and indivisible," and viewed the Hetman state as a transition from the radicalism of 1917 to a restored great Russia. Ironically, it was the Hetman state's liberal policies of refuge that allowed these organizations to survive possible execution or arrest in Bolshevik Russia, but the emerging White movement failed to see the emergence of an independent Ukraine as anything but a German puppet state whose days were limited. Despite Skoropadsky's insistence on his common interests with the leaders of the White movement in the south and Siberia, and his financing and arming of the Don and Kuban' Cossack republics, his intentions were rebuffed and worse. Monarchists and Russian nationalist organizations also plotted against the Hetman and his government. Sometimes, but not always, these White Russian organizations were tied to the numerous espionage nests of the Entente in Ukraine, who sought to recruit both anti-German and anti-Ukrainian activists.[56]

Of course, the hostile neighbor to the north, Soviet Russia, also worked against any stabilization of Skoropadsky's regime in Ukraine, despite promises in the Brest Treaty to Germany and Austria-Hungary that Russia would seek peace with Ukraine and recognize its sovereignty. Bolshevik intelligence agents tried to recruit collaborators in the Hetman's government and entourage, and looked no doubt with approval at the more open efforts of the Socialist-Revolutionary terrorists. All this intrigue and conspiracy contributed to an atmosphere of high insecurity in the immediate entourage of Skoropadsky. Besides the assassination of Eichhorn, a couple of dramatic explosions, particularly that of a gunpowder depot at Zvirnytsi on 6 June, raised the level of anxiety in the capital.[57] This led to concern about the continuity of the Hetman state and resulted in the production of a succession document that sought to guarantee a smooth transition in the event of the death of the Hetman.[58]

As early as June 1918, the German commander of Kiew, Field Marshal Eichhorn, was so frightened by the chaos outside the capital that he did not leave the city once before his own assassination. Even before the defeat of the Central Powers in November 1918, local occupation authorities began planning the eventual evacuation of Ukraine.[59] Reports of growing unrest and loss of control across the land were augmented by alarming news of loss of morale among the occupying troops.[60] Efforts to instill greater patriotism among the soldiers, including the invitation of German professors to lecture the troops and thereby "develop their love of their fatherland" proved of little value. When, finally, the order came for evacuation on 11 November 1918, it marked the beginning of a panicked withdrawal that was harassed along its path by Ukrainian insurgent forces. The Germans and their allies witnessed the decomposition of their army into a force of plunder; soldiers sold their uniforms and weapons, often for alcohol and a good time. By the end of November the entire region west of the Dnipro was in the hands of the rebels, as were the rail connections.[61] The partisans disarmed as many retreating troops as possible and effectively blocked any further transport of valuables out of Ukraine.

The Perspective of a Russian-Ukrainian Patriot: The Hetman's Frustrated State- and Nation-Building under German Occupation

Coup and assassination plots against him and his government notwithstanding, and when the persistent inability to guarantee the Central Powers their promised grain supplies is taken into consideration, it can be argued that Hetman Skoropadsky and his cabinets contributed more to the emergence of a modern Ukraine than did their critical and socialist predecessors and successors in the Rada and Directory governments, especially in the areas of institution-building and international recognition for a sovereign Ukraine.[62] Skoropadsky's memoirs, composed shortly after his flight to Germany from Ukraine in 1918, offer a fascinating counterpoint to the diaries and memoirs of General Groener, with whom he forged a friendship that continued after the occupation in the interwar years, despite Skoropadsky's at best ambivalent attitudes toward Groener's government. By comparing these two men's memories of those years, we can reconstruct the perspectives of both the occupying general and his most important counterpart in the "native" government who was trying desperately to establish his own authority after a coup and his suspension of the elections to the Ukrainian Constituent Assembly. The memoirs also reveal a distinctly different vision of Ukraine from that of Skoropadsky's socialist rivals.

After the Treaty of Brest-Litovsk was signed between the Rada (already no longer in occupation of Bolshevik-held Kyiv) and the Central Powers, Skoropadsky was also forced to reassess his attitudes toward Germany and Austria-Hungary, the occupying powers in Ukraine after January 1918. A clearly defensive tone in his memoirs betrays his sensitivity to charges that he was a German puppet, but also that he had betrayed the Allied cause by his collaboration with the occupying authorities. In particular, Great Russian parties tried to discredit Skoropadsky as a Germanophile.[63] Skoropadsky even felt compelled to distinguish his own program of federalism from the Germans' designs to dismantle the Russian Empire by peeling off its western nations. (After all, he reminded his readers, the Germans were not in favor of Ukraine's adhering to a federation with Russia.)[64] Furthermore, he, together with most of conservative—and a good part of liberal—Russian imperial society, believed that the Bolsheviks were German agents and that the Germans were thereby largely responsible for their coming to power in Russia. A certain measure of his distaste for the Rada lay in his firm suspicion that they were already secretly negotiating with the Germans in late 1917 (particularly Mykola Porsh, who became the Rada's general secretary for military affairs in December 1917).[65] Not surprisingly, Skoropadsky described his attitudes toward and relations with the Germans (and Austrians) with a great deal of ambivalence. He recorded his disgust with the turn of events that made the Germans appear to be saviors of Ukraine (and Russia, by extension) from "the Bolshevik yoke."[66] He was impressed nonetheless with the Germans' orderliness and compared them favorably with their partners, the Austrians. His most positive characterizations are, perhaps not surprisingly, of military men, as contrasted with the diplomats and small armies of civilian "advisors" and economic planners from German business circles. Still, he found it difficult to understand why the German military men took the socialist Rada government so seriously (at least at first) and why they continued to view the Ukrainian Social Democrats and Socialist-Revolutionaries as the only influential Ukrainian parties, and this even after the Germans backed his coup against the Rada. He tied this German support for Ukrainian socialists to their continued support for the Bolsheviks in Petrograd, but came to realize that this pro-Bolshevik policy was the subject of some serious policy disagreements within the German government itself.[67]

Skoropadsky's first contact with representatives of the governments he had only recently been fighting against as a Russian general was in March 1918, when the Austrians announced their plans to take over the hotel in Kyiv/Kiew where Skoropadsky had been staying. At this time, he met with the Austrian ambassador and the Austrian military plenipotentiary, Major Fleischmann, a man Skoropadsky took to be characteristic of Austrian duplicity. He quickly learned in these first contacts that the Germans and Austrians had many serious and frequent conflicts and disagreements over their occupation policy and the war more generally.[68] He traced his first meeting with the German authorities to his request for their help in securing the release of his wife and family, who were still behind Bolshevik lines. (The Germans were able to help in this matter through their contacts in Petrograd and Moscow.)[69] Skoropadsky's most constant contact during 1918 was General Groener, who from March 1918 was chief of staff of army group Kiew. (It was also Groener who directed the German retreat from Kiew; in October 1918 he was appointed to replace General Ludendorff as quartermaster-general.) During April 1918 Skoropadsky's contacts with the Germans became more frequent and they soon began to revolve around the possibility of a coup against the Rada. Interestingly, Skoropadsky kept the details of this plot secret from the Austrian, Major Fleischmann. In the end, he was able to secure the Germans' neutrality during the coup, asking them only to make sure that the Sich Sharpshooters remained confined to their barracks, lest they feel an obligation to defend the Rada government.[70]

All the while, Skoropadsky insisted that he was not a Germanophile by any means, but a Ukrainophile above all. He found his alliance with the Germans troubling and tried to keep doors open to the Entente powers as well, hoping that they would respond to his efforts in creating an anti-Bolshevik *place d'armes* for the recovery of Russia. But the French and British governments gave priority to the Russian White cause and were thereby constrained in the support they could show for Skoropadsky or any autonomous or independent Ukrainian state. Skoropadsky claimed to prefer the Entente not only out of respect for the wartime alliance, but because in the end he expected them to win over Germany. During

1917 Skoropadsky had good relations with French and British officers. In December 1917 France briefly established diplomatic relations with Ukraine; their mission, headed by General Tabouis, had authority over the Polish and Czechoslovak troops in Ukraine, which Skoropadsky hoped might help to defend the Rada in the event of the expected Bolshevik attack. Skoropadsky was negotiating with the French at the same time the Rada was sending its first peace mission to the Germans.[71] After the Rada, now the Ukrainian People's Republic, signed the Treaty of Brest-Litovsk, however, the French mission left Ukraine. Once the Entente cast their lots with the White proto-governments around the peripheries of the former Russian Empire, they were generally hostile to Ukraine's independent existence. Ultimately, he concluded that the Entente also bore a large measure of responsibility for the failure of his state.[72]

Skoropadsky's greatest talents in statecraft lay in the military sphere, but the German and Austrian occupation regime forbade him from exercising those talents until virtually the end of his rule.[73] At first Skoropadsky tried to win permission from the Germans to organize his own armed forces by offering to have those troops collect the grain demanded by the treaty from the Ukrainian population under the terms of the Brest Treaty. The Germans refused, but at least their troops managed to carry out that mission with relative order and efficiency. By contrast, Skoropadsky recalled that the Austrian troops simply pillaged the countryside because they too were beginning to feel the impact of nationalist and Bolshevik "degeneration." The Austrians, moreover, were thoroughly corrupt, and bribery developed in their occupation zone on a "colossal scale."[74] Finally, Skoropadsky was acutely aware of the Austrians' plans to install their own hetman on the throne of Ukraine after they won the war.[75]

Though Skoropadsky was allowed to have an army and naval minister (and even a chief of his general staff), he was not permitted to begin organizing an army. (The Germans seized all the navy in the Black Sea except two armed carriers and only agreed in the fall to return this fleet to the Ukrainian state; they also insisted that the Ukrainians pay for some share of the former Russian fleet!) His own military forces were limited to those that had already been formed by the Ukrainian National Republic and the various Ukrainianized units of the former Russian Army. General Groener insisted that 2000 troops were sufficient for keeping order in Kyiv/Kiew and guarding Skoropadsky. (The combined forces of the German and Austrian armies were estimated at 400,000 on Ukrainian territory.) Moreover, not only had the Germans and the Austrians occupied all the suitable barracks for their own soldiers, but both armies made several attempts of their own at organizing military units from Ukrainian prisoners-of-war in their camps.[76] Although the Hetman was upset by these attitudes, the occupying powers ignored his protests until the bitter end of his regime. And as if German opposition were not enough, his plans for building an army were fought within his own council of ministers. His military advisors nonetheless began drawing up plans and military codes for that day when they might be allowed to actually create the modern army that many imperial officers had dreamed about before World War I broke out.[77] Moreover, the Hetman's intelligence reports about Bolshevik units forming in Chernihiv and Kursk suggested that a new offensive would be launched in spring 1919, so time was running short for organizing conscription and some minimal training of the new Ukrainian army.

Out of desperation over this situation, Skoropadsky began pressing the German occupation authorities in Kyiv/Kiew to arrange an invitation for him from Emperor Wilhelm to visit Germany. Among other matters, Skoropadsky wanted to try to counter what he saw as the pro-Bolshevik orientation of the German Ministry of Foreign Affairs; he believed that German military leadership had already seen the dangers in this policy and concurred with him in his opposition to it.[78] Finally, the emperor was persuaded to receive Hetman Skoropadsky and a Ukrainian delegation on an official visit at the start of September 1918. Emperor Wilhelm bestowed the Order of the Red Eagle on Skoropadsky and recognized the independence of Ukraine in an official speech. Skoropadsky recalled the emperor's attention focused on what Skoropadsky might know about the fate of his imperial Russian in-laws, the Romanovs, now in hostile Bolshevik hands (actually already murdered). From Kassel, Skoropadsky proceeded via Hannover to Spa (in German-occupied Belgium), the headquarters of Field Marshal Hindenburg and Ludendorff. (On the way, he was troubled to observe the decline of the German army.) For the little it was worth in the end, Skoropadsky was relieved to learn that both high commanders were against the Bolshevik orientation and favored his efforts to build a Ukrainian army. Skoropadsky's experience with the rise of socialists in Russia in 1917 made him very aware that leftists were on the rise in Germany too; and while he took this as an unfortunate omen, he recognized that he might have to deal with a new German government before long and requested his deputy foreign minister to ascertain which of the German socialists were "worth getting to know" for the future. From the army he visited the Kiel naval residence of Prince Henry of Prussia, brother of the emperor. Princess Irene was the sister of Russian Empress Alexandra and repeated her brother-in-law's inquiries about their relatives' fate. Once again, Skoropadsky was troubled by the restive mood of the German sailors he saw in Kiel, which evoked unpleasant memories of 1917.[79]

Much to his own surprise, Skoropadsky's trip to Germany was greeted as a victory by the Ukrainian parties, who viewed it as a sign of the international recognition of Ukraine. Predictably, the Russian parties viewed it as further evidence of Skoropadsky's treason against Russia. In any event, whatever genuine achievements he might have won in Ukraine's case for greater autonomy and self-government proved to be short-lived in the wake of the November revolution in Germany and the signing of the armistice treaty acknowledging German defeat in the war. Skoropadsky assigned great importance almost from the start to diplomatic relations and the winning of international recognition for his new government; here he had modest success. Germany recognized the government of Ukraine in August, following the ratification of the Brest Treaty in Vienna. Recognition followed from German allies: Austria-Hungary, Turkey, and Bulgaria. Newly independent states or proto-states once part of the Russian Empire also extended diplomatic recognition: the Don and Kuban' Cossacks, Georgia, Finland, and Poland.[80] The historian Dmytro Doroshenko became foreign minister over German objections (they suspected him of Austrian sympathies!).[81] Skoropadsky appointed his future court historian and political theorist Viacheslav Lypynsky as ambassador to Austria-Hungary in June 1918; and Baron Teodor Shtengel' as ambassador to Germany.[82]

Despite all his misgivings about both the Germans and the Central Rada that negotiated the Brest-Litovsk Treaty, he never thought to renounce it. He realized that he needed the good will of the Germans and Austrians. The Germans and Austrians already had appointed ambassadors to the Rada government in Ukraine and they remained after the coup. Skoropadsky spent the first days of his Hetmancy in frequent contact with the German Oberkommando, Field Marshal Eichhorn, the German Ambassador Mumm, and his Austrian counterpart Ritter von Herwilt Princig.[83] These institutional relations, as well as the important trip to Germany in late fall 1918, brought the Hetman into constant contact with the occupiers, and he recorded his evolving understanding of them. He divided the Germans with whom he came in contact in Ukraine into three large categories. The first was the "military class," whom he recalled as "honest," in many cases "democrats by conviction" who did not want Ukraine's ruin, who tried to understand Ukraine, "but relied on books published in L'viv" and were at the mercy of Ukrainian chauvinists." He also observed the lamentable decline in the German officer corps very soon after the November revolution in Germany, drawing obvious parallels to what he had observed more closely in the Russian Army. The second group consisted of diplomats, who, "like all diplomats, adapted to their ministry, the emperor and his circle, the Reichstag, and eventually even the socialists." The diplomats arrived with all sorts of experts in finance, industry, and trade, and societies to explore Ukrainian resources with an eye to grandiose projects. Finally, the third group included representatives of German culture and scholarship--various specialists, scholars, and journalists. Skoropadsky expressed his disappointment after the high esteem in which he had held German scholarship and culture confronted "firm prejudices" and "little account of reality." He also observed that the assassination of the German Field Marshal Hermann von Eichhorn at the end of July seriously shook the entire German community.[84] Skoropadsky's closest German colleague, General Groener, conceded that Germany's unwise policies in eastern Europe were also very much to blame for Ukraine's failure.[85]

Preliminary Conclusions

The Great War proved especially destructive and transformative for the peoples of the territories on the borderlands between Germany, Austria-Hungary, and the Russian Empire, where most of the fighting occurred: Poles, Jews, Ukrainians, Belorussians, and the Baltic peoples, but also for the three peoples whose imperial military elites unleashed this war—the Russians, Germans and Austrians.[86] And yet, over the course of the war, the attitudes of the central political authorities toward engaging with "the national question" evolved, above all in the Russian case, in the direction of acknowledging, whether reluctantly or not, the principle of national self-determination. This accommodation was forced on the capitals not only by most of the socialist democracies in the national regions, but also by the American President Woodrow Wilson in the international sphere in his "Fourteen Points." The occupation regimes also united the two Ukraines for the first time in modern history and raised the hopes of activists in the Ukrainian national movement that the time had arrived to realize their ambitions of building a new, independent nation out of the imperial rivalries.

Overseeing the occupation, however, proved to be unexpectedly challenging for all sides in the conflict. On the side of the Central Powers, from early on tensions plagued the efforts of Austria-Hungary and Germany to coordinate their actions; for that matter, Austrian and Hungarian officials very often pursued separate aims in the war. Russians heard frequent criticism from their French and British allies, but also from the international Jewish community and the Vatican. Foreign ministry officials tended to clash with the military authorities over how to divide power in the best interests of both the short and long term. Other bureaucracies also pursued their own agendas in the occupied regions, from finance to agriculture to "settlement"—and to colonial offices in the German case, and the Holy Synod in the Russian case. Even within ministries, especially for foreign affairs and the military, there were often severe differences between the capitals (Berlin, Vienna, Petrograd) and the ministry's own representatives on the ground, who had many times been sent there because they were that ministry's experts on the region. It was not uncommon for local representatives to protest decisions—often in vain—that were based on what they perceived to be poor understanding of local conditions.

In several cases, the occupying authorities had their missions further complicated by a change in regime that affected their ground operations. During the second Russian occupation, the Romanov dynasty was replaced by a liberal-centrist coalition government in Petrograd and more radical counterparts in Kyiv. The Germans, too, started their second occupation regime with the Rada socialists, but proceeded to change the regime in favor of more conservative and less democratic politicians with the Ukrainian Hetmanate of Pavlo Skoropadsky. Also in the German case, although the official regime change would come in November 1918, the increasing pressure of the liberal-socialist opposition in the *Reichstag* helped shape occupation policies. With each change of regime, occupation policies also changed significantly, though by 1917–1918 the situation in Ukraine quickly grew beyond the control of any authority, whether in Petrograd, Kyiv, or Berlin. The history of the Rada/Ukrainian National Republic and Skoropadsky's Ukrainian State offer stark illustrations of the challenges and limits of nation- and state-building under foreign occupation and during wartime.

The deterioration of all three imperial armies, marked by desertion and fraternization on the front lines starting in 1916, fed and in turn was fed by the rising antiwar sentiment in civilian society as well. Ironically, then, even when the occupying regimes seemed to "learn" lessons from their past mistakes and miscalculations, the changes they introduced could do little to offset the broader international and local developments that led to the collapse of all the imperial powers and their replacement by a series of new states, proto-states, and military-political movements. After the German and Austrian defeat in 1918, the international war took on much more the character of civil war, so that the next rounds of occupations of Ukraine would be fought between Bolshevik Russia, White Russia, newly created independent, irredentist Poland, and the remnants of the Ukrainian movements that survived the prior four years of devastation. The years 1919 and 1920 were dominated by further regime changes in Kyiv, Kharkiv, and L'viv, with Ukraine now in the grip of warlords and arbitrary violence. Yet each new invader or occupier came with the rhetoric of liberation, often national liberation, which inevitably meant punishing some parts of the population and rewarding others. And beyond this, the tragedy of the occupation experience meant the constant meddling of outside powers and the unwillingness and inability of the international community more broadly to see beyond their own national self-interests, however confused and often contradictory they were, for the benefit of the local populations under their dominion.

The consequence of these years of war, revolution, civil war, and occupation was the destruction of most of Ukrainian civil society under both former empires, and the repartition of Ukraine into Polish and Soviet lands. And so the same war that made the rise of a modern Ukrainian state—or states—possible was also the war that doomed those states to failure in the conditions of anarchy, warlordism, famine, and terror that the violence of international conflict unleashed in the summer of 1914. Much of the Ukrainian leadership that survived these terrible years went into exile in Europe and beyond; many others cast their lot with continuing the cause under their new occupiers in Moscow and Warsaw. Both were to experience a difficult future.

NOTES

1. For a German perspective on this from the commander of the occupation forces in Ukraine, see the memoirs of General Wilhelm Groener, *Lebenserinnerungen*, ed. Friedrich Freiherr Hiller von Gaertringen (Goettingen: Vandenhoeck & Ruprecht, 1957), pp. 385–418; the source I rely on most is a selection of his wartime diaries covering the Ukrainian period in Winfried Baumgart, *Von Brest-Litovsk zur deutschen Novemberrevolution* (Goettingen: Vandenhoeck & Ruprecht, 1971), pp. 257–451; Groener's daughter also earlier published extracts from his diaries and letters home to his wife in Dorothea Groener-Geyer, *General Groener. Soldat und Staatsmann* (Frankfurt am Main: Societäts-Verlag, 1954). For secondary literature on Groener's occupation policies in Ukraine, see Winfried Baumgart, "General Groener und die deutsche Besatzungspolitik in der Ukraine 1918," *Geschichte in Wissenschaft und Unterricht* 21 (1970): 325–340; and Baumgart, *Deutsche Ostpolitik. Von Brest-Litowsk bis zum Ende des Ersten Weltkrieges* (Wien, München, Oldenbourg, 1966). For the Austrian points of view, see Hornykiewicz, *Ereignisse*, III.
2. For a standard English-language treatment of the Treaty and the negotiations surrounding it, see John Wheeler-Bennett, *Brest-Litovsk: The Forgotten Peace, March 1918* (London: Macmillan, 1938); for the negotiations between the Ukrainian Hetman State and the Russian Soviet Republic, including previously unpublished documents, see Yaroslav Pelensky and others, eds., *Myrni perehovory mizh Ukrains'koiu Derzhavoiu ta RSFRR 1918 r.* (Kyiv/New York/Philadelphia: Vydavnytstvo M. P. Kots', 1999).
3. Murav'ev was an officer in the imperial army before joining the Left SRs during 1917 and becoming an ally and collaborator with the Bolsheviks until he turned his troops against the Bolsheviks in support of the Left SR uprising in Moscow during the summer of 1918. He was killed in Simbirsk.
4. Groener's diary entry, March 20, in Baumgart, *Von Brest-Litovsk*, pp. 307–308.
5. For contemporary accounts of the Murav'ev occupation, see A. A. Gol'denveizer, "Iz kievskikh vospominanii," pp. 24–26; S. Sumskii, "Odinnadtsat' perevorotov," pp. 98–105; in S. A. Alekseev, ed., *Revoliutsiia na Ukraine* (Moscow/Leningrad: Gosudarstvennoe izdatel'stvo, 1930). Gol'denveizer recalls that one positive side of the German occupation was the restoration of ties to Europe, in particular German-speaking Europe, for the first time since the war started. The Germans opened two bookstores that received newspapers from Vienna and Berlin. One of the other "achievements" along these lines was the establishment of regular rail service between Kyiv/Kiew and Berlin.
6. General Alexander von Linsingen, cited in Baumgart, *Von Brest-Litovsk*, p. 260n.
7. Even before he arrived in Kyiv, Groener had the impression that the Rada government was "at the moment a speck in the firmament; who, where, what, and how this government functioned was not clear to anyone; all that was clear was that we had to make this government capable of ruling through our authority and power, but to maintain the fiction that the Rada was the real power." Diary entry, 1 March, in Baumgart, *Von Brest-Litovsk*, p. 263. This impression was reinforced by his dealings with the government once he arrived. In fact, though, he was frustrated by the general ignorance in German military circles about Ukraine's situation; see pp. 262–263, 265, 268.

8. Groener letter to Oldershausen, 19 March, pp. 302–303; Draft letter to Ludendorff, 22 March, p. 317; Letter to Ludendorff, 23 March, p. 319. Because of the immense tasks that the German army had before it and his estimation of the low numbers, Groener acknowledged that the Austrian partners, whom he refers to often as *Buendnisbrueder* (alliance brothers), were indispensable, however many objections there might be from German and Ukrainian authorities.

9. Dmytro Doroshenko, *History of Ukraine, 1917–1923*, Vol. II (The Ukrainian Hetman State of 1918), trans. D. M. Elcheshen (Toronto: The Basilian Press, 1973), pp. 28–29.

10. *Die deutsche Okkupation der Ukraine. Geheimdokumente* (Strasbourg: Editions Promethee, 1937), docs. 32–35, pp. 86–91, July 1918.

11. *Die deutsche Okkupation*, doc. 77, Emperor Karl to Archprince Wilhelm, May 1918, p. 181.

12. Groener was relieved that the Austrians didn't pretend to take the Rada seriously and wished his government would take a similarly "realistic" approach. Diary entry, 20 March, in Baumgart, *Von Brest-Litovsk*, pp. 305–306. Groener was particularly impressed by the new Austrian ambassador to Kyiv/Kiew, Count Johann Nepomuk Gabriel Forgach, who similarly expressed his agreement with Groener in his own reports to Vienna. Ibid., pp. 314–315n.

13. *Die deutsche Okkupation*, doc. 29, 13 June 1918, pp. 79–82. See also the report of Major-General Waldstaetten of the Austrian General Staff to the Foreign Office, in which he surveys the leading figures in Ukrainian politics and identifies them as either friendly to Austria or Germany. The overwhelming majority he discusses are of "German orientation," making Austria's efforts in Kiew very difficult. Waldstaetten could only hope that a change in the current Rada government would work to Austria's advantage. See *Die deutsche Okkupation*, doc. 53, 16 April 1918, pp. 130–135.

14. Groener reports the position of Robert von Langer of the Austrian War Ministry, but he (Groener) was also demanding the resignation of his own immediate superior, General Alexander von Linsingen, because without more authority to make decisions on the ground he felt his hands were tied. Diary entry, 19 March, p. 300. Groener also frequently appealed to his superiors to work out an effective relationship with the Austrians because the confusion that characterized the relationship was hindering even the basic task of organizing the grain deliveries. Letter to Oldershausen, 19 March, pp. 302–303.

15. *Die deutsche Okkupation*, doc. 7, 29 March 1918, pp. 34–36; Doroshenko, II, pp. 287–288n.

16. *Die deutsche Okkupation*, doc. 80, Ohnesseit, German Consul-General in Odessa, to Hertling, 20 July 1918, pp. 186–187.

17. *Die deutsche Okkupation*, doc. 78, Appointment of General Krauss as Commander-in-Chief of Ostarmee in Ukraine by Chief of Austrian General Staff, 18 May 1918, pp. 182–183.

18. *Die deutsche Okkupation*, doc. 79, Mumm to Foreign Office, 1 June 1918, pp. 184–185. Mumm noted with indignation that von Boeltz hadn't even bothered to check in with General Eichhorn, the most important German in Ukraine.

19. *Die deutsche Okkupation*, doc. 81, Ohnesseit, German Consul-General in Odessa, to Hertling, 8 August 1918, pp. 188–189. Ohnesseit expressed satisfaction that Gerbel (Serhii Herbel), the Ukrainian Minister of Provisions, had "been healed of his prior prejudice for Austria." He was further pleased that Herbel shared his (and general German) opinion of the Austrians as sloppy (*Schlamperei*) and their officers as more traders and speculators than soldiers; doc. 82, Ambassador Mumm from Kiew reported similarly, and with similar *Schadenfreude*, that the Hetman was growing increasingly anti-Austrian in his orientation, the more contact he had with them. Mumm to Hertling, 10 August, 1918, pp. 190–191.
20. *Die deutsche Okkupation*, doc. 62, General Krauss to Austrian Chief of General Staff, July 1918, pp. 151–153. Groener cites the opinion of a Russian (-German) Baron Wolf von der Osten-Sacken, who was a delegate of the Red Cross in Ukraine, that "the Ukrainians were too unintelligent and indolent to be able to build a state." Diary entry 10 March, in Baumgart, *Von Brest-Litovsk*, p. 290.
21. Groener, diary entries, 5 and 9 March, in Baumgart, *Von Brest-Litovsk*, pp. 273, 287.
22. *Die deutsche Okkupation*, doc. 2, Order of Commander of German Division in Kremenetz, 28 February 1918.
23. Sumskii, "Odinnadtsat' perevorotov," p. 109.
24. Gol'denveizer, "Iz kievskikh vospominanii," pp. 26–29; Sumskii, "Odinnadtsat' perevorotov," pp. 105–109.
25. *Die deutsche Okkupation*, doc 4, 22 March 1918, Ambassador Forgach to Foreign Office (A-H).
26. See *Die deutsche Okkupation*, doc. 3 from Foreign Office representative in Brest-Litvosk, doc. 4 from German General Groener, 31 March 1918 (also Hornykiewicz, *Ereignisse*, I, doc. 133, pp. 326–327) and 9 from Austrian General Langer, 3 April 1918. Groener wrote to Ludendorff complaining about the lack of planning for the economy.
27. See the proclamation of 1 March 1918.
28. The Central Powers insisted on deliveries of one million tons of grain, but the Ukrainian delegation protested this and compromise wording was found to the effect that "excess products" would be offered in exchange for the military protection of the state. *Die deutsche Okkupation*, doc. 1, Czernin to Prime Minister of Austria-Hungary, 5 February 1918. See also Hornykiewicz, *Ereignisse*, vol. II, doc. 209, pp. 38–39.
29. Doroshenko, II, pp. 26–30, citing report of Field Marshal Langer; see also letter of General Groener to his wife, where he complains that "[w]hoever has experienced the loss of reason and incapacity of the socialist rule in Ukraine and the traces of Bolshevism that one sees all around, can not do otherwise than to support the anti-Bolshevik elements;" and his report to Ludendorff on 23 March: "Our policy is to walk on eggshells around the Ukrainian government, which has not earned this name and has no roots in the people. The bureaucratic apparatus is completely destroyed, highly unreliable and in no way capable of rapid work. Austria Hungary sees the situation much more practically; I was interested to hear that the Ukrainian government is only a "coat" (*Mantel*) and that we must do everything else ourselves. We urgently need more troops for these wide spaces, otherwise our authority will be squandered and any practical work is impossible. The attitude of the population is generally against us. In favor of us are the large landholders and capitalists, if we help them to recover their property. Otherwise they too will be against us. Among

the peasants the irritable attitude is bitterer by the day and will come to conflicts because the old ruble has lost its purchasing power for the troops. We have no coal; without it, which is to be found only in the Donets region, the Ukrainian state will remain dependent on Great Russia. And [Russia] will not freely let this region go to Ukraine. If Ukraine receives no coal from the Donets basin, we will have to bring coal [to Ukraine] from across the Danube and from Poland. The peasants will be able to deliver the spring order only minimally, since the socialist program of land division not only threw out all property relations but gave a prize to the laziness of the peasants." In Baumgart, *Von Brest-Litvosk*, pp. 316–319.

30. *Die deutsche Okkupation*, doc. 16, Mumm to Foreign Office, 16 April 1918, pp. 50–51. Still, Ambassador Mumm reported that he sympathized with General Groener "who sees everything falling apart and can not stand by doing nothing."

31. *Die deutsche Okkupation*, doc. 9, Foreign Ministry of Austria-Hungary to Forgach, 3 March 1918 (Hornykiewicz, *Ereignisse* I, doc. 145, pp. 351–352); also Hornykiewicz, ibid., I, doc. 147, pp. 355–358, 4 April 1918.

32. *Die deutsche Okkupation*, doc. 11, Mumm to Foreign Office, 5 April 1918, p. 42.

33. Groener was confident he would have the real authority and power because Eichhorn, although a general Groener respected greatly, was 70 years old and short on energy at this stage of his career. See diary entry, 29 March, letters to wife, 29 and 31 March, in Baumgart, *Von Brest-Litovsk*, pp. 332–333.

34. *Die deutsche Okkupation*, docs. 13, Foreign Office to Mumm, 2 April 1918, p. 44; 12, Foreign Office to Mumm, 11 April 1918, p. 43.

35. *Die deutsche Okkupation*, doc. 14, Austro-Hungarian Representative in Warsaw, Ugron, to Foreign Office, 1 May 1918, p. 45 (Hornykiewicz, *Ereignisse*, II, doc. 365, pp. 331–332); also Doroshenko, II, p. 25.

36. Gol'denveizer, "Iz kievskikh vospominanii," pp. 28–29; Sumskii, "Odinnadtsat' perevorotov," pp. 107–109.

37. Doroshenko, II, pp. 34–35.

38. *Die deutsche Okkupation*, doc. 15, Mumm to Foreign Office, April 1918, pp. 48–49; doc. 18, Mumm to Foreign Office, 19 April 1918, pp. 54–55.

39. Doroshenko, II, pp. 49–50, 169–170 n. *Die deutsche Okkupation*, doc. 19, Mumm to Foreign Office, 24 April 1918, pp. 56–57; doc. 27, Order of Eichhorn, 22 May 1918, pp. 74–76; see also Austrian report on the meeting, Hornykiewicz, *Ereignisse*, I, pp. 400–402.

40. Doroshenko, II, p. 52n; *Die deutsche Okkupation*, doc. 21, Order of Eichhorn on Military Field Courts, 25 April 1918, p. 59.

41. *Die deutsche Okkupation*, doc. 22, 29 April 1918, Mumm to Reichskanzler Hertling, pp. 60–65. For local reaction to the Dobryi "kidnapping," see Gol'denveizer, "Iz kievskikh vospominanii," pp. 32–33; Sumskii, "Odinnadtsat' perevorotov," pp. 112–113.

42. *Die deutsche Okkupation*, doc. 23, Mumm to the Foreign Office, 2 May 1918, pp. 68–69; doc. 24, Eichhorn to Obost, 4 May 1918, pp. 70–71; doc. 25, Foreign Office to Mumm, 8 May 1918, p. 72; doc. 26, Mumm to Foreign Office, 9 May 1918, p. 73.

43. See his "Hramota to all Ukrainian People;" and "Laws Respecting the Provisional State Structure of Ukraine," 29 April 1918, Doroshenko, II, pp. 70–75.

44. *Die deutsche Okkupation*, doc. 28, 3 May 1918, draft of order, pp. 77–78.

45. See an early outline of the organizational plan, in *Die deutsche Okkupation*, doc. 36, Mumm to Reichskanzler Hertling, March 1918, pp. 96–97; the plan was finally approved in early April 1918, doc. 38, Mumm to Foreign Office and Imperial Economics Office, p. 99; but really only got set up and running later in the summer; see doc. 48, "Verzeichnis der Haupt- und Nebenstellen des Staatsgetreidebueros," 3 August 1918, pp. 114–115.

46. *Die deutsche Okkupation*, doc. 39, Mumm to Hertling, 12 April 1918, p. 99; doc. 46, German memorandum of concern about upcoming negotiations of Ukraine with Soviet Russia, 1 June 1918, pp. 109–110.

47. *Die deutsche Okkupation*, doc. 40, Mumm to Foreign Office and Economic Office, 3 May 1918, p. 101. The Germans, incidentally, expressed their agreement with the Austrian position.

48. *Die deutsche Okkupation*, doc. 45, German General Consul in Odessa to Foreign Office, 20 May 1918, pp. 107–108; Ohnesseit reported that Kherson and Tauride provinces were particularly restless because the peasants understood the Hetman to have reneged on the earlier agrarian policy of allowing land seizures from the gentry.

49. *Die deutsche Okkupation*, doc. 42, Foreign Office to Mumm, 30 April 1918, p. 103; the Foreign Office reported to Mumm that "German capital and labor" were ready to help in raising up Ukraine's devastated economy; see the request of the chamber of commerce of Harburg, a major producer of submarine parts for the Imperial Navy, to the Kyiv embassy regarding the trip of iron and bronze work executive Robert Koeber to Ukraine, doc. 51, Harburg Chamber of Commerce to Mumm, 29 August 1918, pp. 122–123.

50. *Die deutsche Okkupation*, doc. 43, Mumm to Foreign Office, May 1918, p. 104.

51. *Die deutsche Okkupation*, doc. 47, German Interior Ministry to Foreign Office, 14 July 1918, pp. 111–113. This project was inspired by the German General Electric Company, which had been planning air routes to counter Sweden's plans to introduce London–Stockholm–St. Petersburg lines.

52. During one of prime minister Fedir Lyzohub's first meetings with Ambassador Mumm, he asked if the level of support by the Germans for the new government remained as high as it had been at its inception; Mumm suggested that the government ought to exhibit more "couleur locale" and include more "Ukrainian elements." Lyzohub protested, citing all the new government had done to encourage use of the Ukrainian language in government. *Die deutsche Okkupation*, doc. 30, Mumm to Groener, 1 July 1918, pp. 83–84.

53. *Die deutsche Okkupation*, doc. 56, Mumm to Foreign Office, 20 May 1918, p. 139.

54. *Die deutsche Okkupation*, doc. 54, Mumm to Hertling, 8 May 1918, pp. 136–137, discussing Viacheslav Lypynsky's candidacy for Foreign Minister and objections from a representative of the opposition, Mr. Stepankowski. See also doc. 55, Dmytro Doroshenko to Mumm, 10 May 1918, p. 138, defending his own candidacy for the foreign minister's position after other critics complained of his (Doroshenko's) political orientation. Also see the report of a remarkable meeting between Ukrainian party leaders at the residence of General Groener, in which Mykola Mikhnovsky demanded changes in the Hetman's overly Russian cabinet; doc. 58, 10 June 1918, pp. 142–147.

55. A day after the 30 July 1918 assassination of Eichhorn in Kiew, the only day that Groener had not been accompanying him (due to an operation on a boil on the back of his neck), he wrote his wife, "What a hard day is behind me! I was unable to write you yesterday. Meanwhile the telegraph transmitted the sad news of the murder of General Field Marshal von Eichhorn to the whole world. The assassin was sent from the left SRs in Moscow, the same ones who murdered Count Mirbach. [. . .] The murder of Eichhorn has affected me deeply. Since I accompanied him daily at his table in his residence, I could have met the same fate as he did if I had not been bound to my room on that day for medical reasons. The death of Eichhorn is an irreplaceable loss, because he was the only one who, in the event of a change in the OHL, because of his outstanding mental abilities, his wisdom and his strategic and political judgment could be considered [a candidate]." Baumgart, *Von Brest-Litovsk*, pp. 412–413.

56. See Anna Procyk, *Russian Nationalism and Ukraine: The Nationality Policy of the Volunteer Army during the Civil War* (Edmonton and Toronto: Canadian Institute of Ukrainian Studies Press, 1995).

57. See Doroshenko, II, chapter 7, for a survey of the attempts on the lives of high officials and other terrorist acts in the capital, pp. 149–163.

58. "The Provisional Law respecting the Higher State Administration in the event of death, serious illness and absence abroad of His Serene Highness Sir Hetman of All Ukraine," 4 August 1918, Doroshenko, II, pp. 99–102.

59. *Die deutsche Okkupation*, doc. 90, Burian to Forgach, 18 August 1918, p. 203.

60. *Die deutsche Okkupation*, doc. 89, Berchem to Foreign Office, 25 June 1918, p. 202.

61. See G. Frantz, "Die Rueckfuehrung des deutschen Besatzungsheeres aus der Ukraine 1918/19," *Wehr und Wissen* 1934, No. 7.

62. The recent publication of the memoirs of Pavel/Pavlo Skoropadsky/Skoropads'kyi, *Spohady: kinets' 1917–hruden' 1918*, ed. Jaroslaw Pelenski (Kyiv/Philadelphia: National Academy of Sciences of Ukraine, M. S. Hrushevs'kyi Institute of Ukrainian Archeography and Fontology, V. K. Lypynsky East European Research Institute, 1995) sheds new light and offers historians a relatively new perspective on the revolutionary years of 1917–1918 in Ukraine and the Russian Empire more generally. For the first English-language treatment of these materials, as they were being prepared for publication, see Jaroslaw Pelenski, "Hetman Pavlo Skoropadsky and Germany (1917–18) as Reflected in His Memoirs," in Hans-Joachim Torke and John-Paul Himka, eds., *German-Ukrainian Relations in Historical Perspective* (Edmonton and Toronto: Canadian Institute of Ukrainian Studies Press, 1994), pp. 69–83. See also Mark von Hagen, "I Love Russia, but Want Ukraine: How a Russian Imperial General Became Hetman Pavlo Skoropadsky of the Ukrainian State," in *Synopsis: A Collection of Essays in Honor of Zenon E. Kohut*, ed. Frank Sysyn and Serhii Plokhii (Edmonton and Toronto: Canadian Institute of Ukrainian Studies Press, 2005). The memoirs supplement and partly challenge some of the accounts of this period and of Skoropadsky's rule that were based largely on Austrian or German sources or the memoirs of Ukrainian politicians who fought with Skoropadsky for influence over the Ukrainian cause. See the very helpful studies based on these materials by Taras Hunczak, "The Ukraine Under Hetman Pavlo Skoropadskyi," in Hunczak, ed., *The Ukraine, 1917–1921: A Study in Revolution* (Cambridge, MA: Harvard Ukrainian Research Institute, 1977), pp. 61–81; Oleh Fedyshyn, *Germany's Drive to the East and the Ukrainian Revolution, 1917–1918*

(New Brunswick, NJ: Rutgers University Press, 1971); Peter Borowsky, "Germany's Ukrainian Policy during World War I and the Revolution of 1918–19," in Torke and Himka, *German-Ukrainian Relations*, pp. 84–94; and Peter Borowsky, "Deutsche Ukrainepolitik 1918 (unter besonderer Beruecksichtigung der Wirtschaftsfragen." *Historische Studien*, vol. 416 (Luebeck-Hamburg: Matthiesen, 1970).

63. Skoropadsky, *Spohady*, pp. 56, 114.
64. Ibid., p. 51.
65. Ibid., pp. 100, 113.
66. Ibid., pp. 121–122.
67. Ibid., pp. 122–125.
68. Ibid., pp. 130–131, 239–241.
69. Ibid., pp. 135–136; 242–243. Sometime in late December 1917 or early January 1918 the Skoropadsky family estate in Trostianets was burnt to the ground.
70. Ibid., pp. 139–142.
71. Ibid., pp. 47, 64, 67, 102–103, 105.
72. Ibid., pp. 47, 146. His imperial military training left him somewhat proficient in French; in a telling incident, when Skoropadsky finally got his visit to Kaiser Wilhelm in late 1918, he spoke everywhere with his German military and political counterparts in French, since he didn't know German. For those German officers who didn't know French, a translator had to be provided!
73. Skoropadsky recalled that the Germans demanded several conditions before promising their covert support and public neutrality in the event of a coup: (1) that Skoropadsky's new government recognize the Brest Treaty signed between Germany and the Rada government; (2) that Skoropadsky take measures to regulate the Ukrainian currency; (3) that he assure better control over the export of foodstuffs to the Central Powers [this was part of the Brest conditions]; (4) that he put through a law permitting German troops stationed in Ukraine the right to purchase necessary food supplies at local prices; (5) that he delay the convening of the diet (*soim, seim*) until the German authorities felt the situation was stable and favorable; (6) that he restore the judicial system to a measure of functioning "and remove all demagoguish elements"; (7) that free trade be restored; and (8) that Germany have the right to acquire any surpluses beyond those destined for export already. Ibid., p. 148.
74. Ibid., p. 184.
75. Habsburg circles had been preparing one of their own, Archduke Wilhelm von Habsburg-Lothringen, aka Vasyl Vyshyvany (1896–1948), for the throne of an autonomous Ukraine in the victorious Habsburg empire. Wilhelm was the son of archduke Karl; from the age of twelve he had lived with his parents on their estate in Galicia where he had studied the Ukrainian language and been exposed to Ukrainophile ideas. Ibid., pp. 208, 239–41.
76. Ibid., pp. 189–90. The UNR had signed an agreement with Germany in March allowing for Ukrainian POWs to be recruited to for the First Ukrainian Division, the *sinezhupany*, in camps in Rastatt, Wezlar, and Salzwedel.
77. Ibid., pp. 178–79
78. Ibid., pp. 241–242, 269–271. Skoropadsky reported that General Groener kept trying to get his government to break off relations with the Bolsheviks.
79. Ibid., pp. 273–282.
80. Ibid., pp. 265–266.

81. Ibid., p. 162. German objections forced Skoropadsky to appoint Mykola Vasylenko, his minister of popular enlightenment and a prominent Kyiv Kadet professor, as acting minister of foreign affairs for the first few weeks of the Hetmanate.

82. Shtengel' was a member of the Ukrainian fraction of the first State Duma; a member of the Kadet Party, and of the Society of Ukrainian Progressivists who formed the Central Rada; later he joined the Ukrainian Party of Socialist-Federalists.

83. Ibid., pp. 171–172.

84. Ibid., pp. 245–248.

85. On 20 October, he wrote his wife: "I for some time have considered our eastern policy to be not the most reasonable, but we have squandered the psychological moment for new political directions. The war is a chain of missed military and political opportunities. . . .The change of ministers (in Ukraine) was made easier after several ministers made public in the press their Great Russian sentiments; I don't take it for so bad since our policy was not likely to win any particular love for Germany from Great Russian patriots. If the people did not want to know anything about the dismemberment of Russia and inclined to the Entente, that too is understandable, since it was WE who signed the Brest peace with the Bolsheviks and who have remained their friends. With such a policy we can hardly expect any love from the right-wing Russian parties." Dorothea Groener, *General Groener*, p. 86–87.

86. For the plight of the Jews during the Great War, see Heinz-Dietrich Loewe, *Antisemitismus und reaktionaere Utopie: Russischer Konservatismus im Kampf gegen den Wandel von Staat und Gesellschaft, 1890–1917* (Hamburg: Hoffmann und Campe Verlag, 1978), chapter VIII; on the Baltic peoples, see Vejas Liulevicius, *War Land on the Eastern Front: Culture, National Identity, and German Occupation in World War I* (Cambridge, UK: Cambridge University Press, 2000).

BIBLIOGRAPHY and SOURCES

Archives

Russian State Military-History Archive (Abbreviated as RGVIA), f. 1759;
f. 2000; f. 2003; f. 2067.

National Archives of Canada. "The Andry Zhuk Collection." MG 30,
C 167, vols. 8, 9, 10, 12, 13.

Hoover Institution Archives. Rerberg, Fedor. "Istoricheskie tainy velikikh
pobed i porazhenii, predatel'stva i revoliutsii. Desiatyi armeiskii korpus
na poliakh srazhenii pervogo perioda Velikoi Voiny." Unpublished
manuscript, 1925.

Newspaper

Armeiskii vestnik, 1915. L'vov.

Published Documents

Browder, Robert Paul, and Alexander F. Kerensky. *The Russian
Provisional Government 1917, documents.* Vols. I and II. Stanford,
CA: Stanford University Press, 1961.

Die deutsche Okkupation der Ukraine. Geheimdokumente. Strasbourg:
Editions Prométhée, 1937.

Golder, F. A., ed. *Documents of Russian History, 1914–1917.* New York:
The Century Company, 1927.

Hornykiewicz, Theophil, ed. *Ereignisse in der Ukraine 1914–1922 deren
Bedeutung und historische Hintergruende.* 4 vols. Philadelphia:
Ferdinand Berger Printing House, 1966.

*Sovet ministrov Rossiiskoi Imperii v gody pervoi mirovoi voiny. Bumagi
A. N. Iakhontova (Zapisi zasedanii i perepiska).* St. Petersburg:
Dmitrii Bulanin, 1999.

Ukrains'ka Tsentral'na Rada: Dokumenty i materially. 2 vols. Kyiv:
Naukova Dumka, 1996.

BIBLIOGRAPHY and SOURCES

Unpublished theses and dissertations.

Hoffman, Jerry Hans. "The Ukrainian Adventure of the Central Powers." Ph.D. dissertation University of Pittsburgh, 1967.

Smolynec, Gregory. "The Union for the Liberation of Ukraine, 1914–1918." Master's thesis, Carleton University, Ottawa, ON, 1993.

Books and Articles.

Armstrong, John. "Mobilized and Proletarian Diasporas." *The American Political Science Review* 70 (1976): 393–408.

Bachmann, Klaus. *"Ein Herd der Feindschaft gegen Russland". Galizien als Krisenherd in den Beziehungen der Donaumonarchie mit Russland (1907–1914).* Munich: R. Oldenbourg Verlag, 2001.

Bakhturina, A. Iu. *Politika Rossiiskoi Imperii v Vostochnoi Galitsii v gody Pervoi mirovoi voiny.* Moscow: AIRO-XX, 2000.

Baumgart, Winfried. *Deutsche Ostpolitik. Von Brest-Litowsk bis zum Ende des Ersten Weltkrieges.* Wien, München: Oldenbourg Verlag, 1966.

———. "General Groener und die deutsche Besatzungspolitik in der Ukraine 1918." *Geschichte in Wissenschaft und Unterricht* 21 (1970): 325–340.

———. *Von Brest-Litovsk zur deutschen Novemberrevolution.* Goettingen: Vandenhoeck & Ruprecht, 1971.

Beloi, A. *Galitsiiskaia bitva.* Moscow and Leningrad: Gosizdat, 1929.

Bihl, Wolfdieter. "Einige Aspekte der oesterreichisch-ungarischen Ruthenenpolitik 1914–1918," pp. 539–550. In *Jahrbuecher fuer Geschichte Osteuropas*, N.F., XIV (1966).

Bociurkiw, Bohdan Rostyslav. *The Ukrainian Greek Catholic Church and the Soviet State (1939–1950).* Edmonton and Toronto: Canadian Institute of Ukrainian Studies Press, 1996.

Borowsky, Peter. "Germany's Ukrainian Policy during World War I and the Revolution of 1918–19," pp. 84–94. In *German-Ukrainian Relations in Historical Perspective.* Edmonton and Toronto: Canadian Institute of Ukrainian Studies Press (1994).

———. "Deutsche Ukrainepolitik 1918 (unter besonderer Beruecksichtigung der Wirtschaftsfragen)." *Historische Studien* vol. 416 (Luebeck-Hamburg: Matthiesen, 1970).

Bradley, John F. N. *The Czechoslovak Legion in Russia, 1914–1920.* New York: Columbia University Press, 1991.

Brusilov, A. A. *Moi vospominaniia.* Moscow: Voenizdat, 1983.

116

Cherniavsky, Michael. *Prologue to Revolution: Notes of A. N. Iakhontov on the Secret Meetings of the Council of Ministers, 1915.* Upper Saddle River, NJ: Prentice-Hall, 1967.

Chernov, V. *The Great Russian Revolution,* trans. Philip E. Mosely. New York: Russell & Russell, 1966, original publication 1936.

Chlamtacz, Marzell. *Lembergs politische Physiognomie waehrend der russischen Invasion.* Vienna, 1916.

Cholodecki, Josef Bialynia. *Lwow w czasie okupacji rosyjskiej (3 wrzesnia 1914–22 czerwca 1915).* Lwow, 1930.

Cholovskii, A. *L'vov vo vremena russkago vladychestva.* Petrograd, 1915.

Coonrod, Robert W. "The Duma's Attitude toward War-time Problems of Minority Groups." *ASEER* 13 (1954): 30–38.

Cornwall, Mark. *The Undermining of Austria-Hungary: The Battle for Hearts and Minds.* London: Macmillan Press, 2000.

Deak, Istvan. *Beyond Nationalism: A Social and Political History of the Habsburg Officer Corps, 1848–1918* (New York: Oxford University Press, 1990).

Debreczeny, Paul, ed., *American Contributions to the Ninth International Congress of Slavists,* vol. II, pp. 305–324. Columbus, OH: Slavica, 1983.

Diakin, V. S. "Pervaia mirovaia voina i meropriatiia po likvidatsii tak nazyvaemogo nemetskogo zasil'ia," pp. 227–238. In *Pervaia mirovaia voina 1914–1918.* Moscow, 1968.

Doroshenko, Dmytro. *History of Ukraine, 1917–1923,* Vol. II (The Ukrainian Hetman State of 1918), translated by D. M. Elcheshen. Toronto, ON: The Basilian Press, 1973.

——. *Istoriia Ukrainy, 1917–1923 rr.,* Vol. I. 2nd ed. New York: Bulava Publishing Corporation, 1954.

——. *Moi spomyny pro nedavne-mynule 1914–1920.* Munich, 1969.

Dragomiretskii, V. S. *Chekhoslovaki v Rossii 1914–1920.* Paris/Prague, 1928.

Edelman, Robert. *Gentry Politics on the Eve of the Russian Revolution: The Nationalist Party, 1907–1917.* New Brunswick, NJ: Rutgers University Press, 1980.

Eley, Geoff. *Reshaping the German Right: Radical Nationalism and Political Change after Bismarck.* New Haven, CT: Yale University Press, 1980.

Evlogii, Georgievskii. *Put' moei zhizni 1868–1946. Vospominaniia,* ed. T. Manuchina. Paris: YMCA Press, 1947.

Fedyshyn, Oleh S. *Germany's Drive to the East and the Ukrainian Revolution in World War I.* New Brunswick, NJ: Rutgers University Press, 1970.

——. "The Germans and the Union for the Liberation of the Ukraine, 1914–1917," pp. 305–322. In *The Ukraine, 1917–1921: A Study in Revolution.* Cambridge, MA: Harvard Ukrainian Research Institute, 1977.

Ferro, Marc. "La politique des nationalités du gouvernement provisoire (fevrier-octobrier 1917)," *Cahiers du monde russe et sovietique* 2 (1961), 131–165.

Fischer, Fritz. *Germany's Aims in the First World War.* New York: Norton, 1967.

——. *World Power or Decline: The Controversy over "Germany's Aims in the First World War."* New York: Norton, 1974.

Fleischhauer, Ingeborg. *Die Deutschen im Zarenreich: Zwei Jahrhunderte deutsch-russische Kulturgemeinschaft.* Stuttgart: Deutsche Verlags-Anstalt, 1986.

Frantz, G. "Die Rueckfuehrung des deutschen Besatzungsheeres aus der Ukraine 1918/19." *Wehr und Wissen* (1934): No. 7.

Gerus, Oleh W. "The Ukrainian Question in the Russia Dumas, 1906–1917: An Overview." *Studia Ucrainica* 2 (1984): 157–168.

Gessen, I. V., ed. "Dokumenty o presledovanii evreev." *Arkhiv russkoi revoliutsii,* vol. XIX. Moscow: "Terra," (1991): pp. 245–284.

Gol'denveizer, A. A. "Iz kievskikh vospominanii." edited by S. A. Alekseev. *Revoliutsiia na Ukraine.* Moscow and Leningrad: Gosudarstvennoe izdatel'stvo, 1930.

Golovin, N. N. *Iz istorii kampanii 1914 goda na russkom fronte. Galitsiiskaia bitva: pervyi period do 1 sentiabria novago stilia.* Paris: Rodnik, 1930.

——. *Iz istorii kampanii 1914 goda. Dni pereloma Galitsiiskoi bitvy (1-3 sentiabria novago stilia).* Paris: Rodnik, 1940.

Graf, Daniel. "Military Rule Behind the Russian Front, 1914–1917: The Political Ramifications." *Jahrbuecher fuer Geschichte Osteuropas,* Neue Folge, Band 22, Heft 3 (1974).

Grebing, Helga. "Oesterreich-Ungarn und die 'Ukrainische Aktion' 1914–18." *Jahrbuecher fuer Geschichte Osteuropas,* N.F., VII, 3. (1959): pp. 270–296.

Groener, Wilhelm. *Lebenserinnerungen*, ed. Friedrich Freiherr Hiller von Gaertringen. Goettingen: Vandenhoeck & Ruprecht, 1957.

Groener-Geyer, Dorothea. *General Groener. Soldat und Staatsmann.* Frankfurt am Main: Societäts-Verlag, 1954.

Hardy, Peter S., ed. *Talergofskii Al'manakh. Propamiatnaia kniga avstriiskikh zhestokostei, izuverstv i nasilii nad karpato-russkim narodom vo vremia vsemirnoi voiny 1914–1917 gg.* L'vov: Izdanie "Talergofskogo komiteta," 1924–1934.

———., ed. *Voennye prestupleniia Gabsburgskoi Monarkhii 1914–1917 gg. Galitskaia Golgofa, Kniga 1.* Trumbull, CT: Hardy Lane, 1964.

Himka, John-Paul. "The Greek Catholic Church and Nation-Building in Galicia, 1772–1918." *Harvard Ukrainian Studies* vol. 8, December (1984), pp. 426–452.

———. *Religion and Nationality in Western Ukraine: The Greek Catholic Church and the Ruthenian National Movement in Galicia.* Montreal, QC: McGill-Queen's University Press, 1999.

Hunczak, Taras. "The Ukraine Under Hetman Pavlo Skoropadskyi." In *The Ukraine, 1917–1921: A Study in Revolution*, pp. 61–81. Cambridge, MA: Harvard Ukrainian Research Institute, 1977.

Iakhontov, A. N. *Prologue to Revolution: Notes of A. N. Iakhontov on the Secret Meetings of the Council of Ministers, 1915*, ed. M. Cherniavsky. Upper Saddle River, NJ: Prentice-Hall, 1967.

"Iz 'chernoi knigi' russkago evreistva, materialy dlia istorii voiny, 1914–1915," *Evreiskaia Starina*, vol. X (1918): pp. 231–253.

Janusz, Bohdan. *Dokumenty urzedowe okupacyi rosyjskiej.* Lwow, 1916.

———. *293 dni rzadow rosyjskich we Lwowie.* Lwow, 1915.

———. *Odezwy i rozporzadzenia z czasow okupacyi rosyjskiej Lwowa, 1914–1915.* Lwow, 1916.

Knox, Alfred. *With the Russian Army, 1914–1917.* 2 vols. New York: Dutton, 1921.

Lasswell, Harold D. *Propaganda Technique in World War I.* New York: P. Smith, 1927.

Lemke, M. K. *250 dnei v tsarskoi Stavke.* Minsk: Kharvest, 2003.

Levyts'kyi, Kost'. *Istoriia politychnoi dumky halyts'kykh ukraintsiv 1848–1914.* 2 vols. L'viv: p.a., 1926.

Lincoln, W. Bruce. *Passage Through Armageddon: The Russians in War and Revolution.* New York: Simon & Schuster, 1986.

Liulevicius, Vejas. *War Land on the Eastern Front: Culture, National Identity, and German Occupation in World War I*. Cambridge, UK: Cambridge University Press, 2000.

Loewe, Heinz-Dietrich. *Antisemitismus und reaktionaere Utopie: Russischer Konservatismus im Kampf gegen den Wandel von Staat und Gesellschaft, 1890–1917*. Hamburg: Hoffmann und Campe Verlag, 1978.

Lohr, Eric. *Nationalizing the Russian Empire: The Campaign against Enemy Aliens during World War I*. Cambridge, MA: Harvard University Press, 2003.

Lotots'kyi, O. *Storinky mynuloho*, Vol. III. Warsaw: Ukrainskyi Naukovyi Instytut, 1934.

Magocsi, Paul Robert. "Old Ruthenianism and Russophilism: A New Conceptual Framework for analyzing National Ideologies in Late Nineteenth Century Eastern Galicia." In Paul Debreczeny, ed., *American Contributions to the Ninth International Congress of Slavists*, vol. II, pp. 305–324. Columbus, OH: Slavica, 1983.

Meyer, Klaus. *Theodor Schiemann als Publizist*. Frankfurt am Main: Rütten & Loening, 1956.

Miller, Alexei. *Imperiia Romanovykh i natsionalizm*. Moscow: Novoe literaturnoe obozrenie, 2006.

——. *"Ukrainskii vopros" v politike vlastei i russkom obshchestvennom mnenii (vtoraia polovina XIX v.)*. Sankt-Peterburg: Aleteia, 2000.

Nelipovich, Sergei. "General ot infanterii N. N. Ianushkevich: 'Nemetskuiu pakost' uvolit' i bez nezhnostei: deportatsii v Rossii 1914–1918 gg." *Voenno-istoricheskii zhurnal* 1 (1997): 42–53.

Pelenski, Jaroslaw. "Hetman Pavlo Skoropadsky and Germany (1917–18) as Reflected in His Memoirs." In Hans-Joachim Torke and John-Paul Himka, eds, *German-Ukrainian Relations in Historical Perspective*, pp. 69–83. Edmonton and Toronto: Canadian Institute of Ukrainian Studies Press, 1994.

Pelensky, Yaroslav ed. *Myrni perehovory mizh Ukrains'koiu Derzhavoiu ta RSFRR 1918 r*. Kyiv/New York/Philadelphia: Vydavnytstvo M. P. Kots', 1999.

Petrovych, Ivan. *Halychyna pidchas rosiis'koi okupatsii: serpen' 1914-cherven' 1915*. L'viv: Politychna Biblioteka, 1915.

Procyk, Anna, *Russian Nationalism and Ukraine: The Nationality Policy of the Volunteer Army during the Civil War*. Edmonton and Toronto: Canadian Institute of Ukrainian Studies Press, 1995.

Przysiecki, Feliks. *Rzady rosyjskie w Galicyi wschodniej*. Piotrkow: Wyd. "Wiadomosci Polskich," 1915.

Rachamimov, Alon. *POWs and the Great War: Captivity on the Eastern Front*. Oxford and New York: Berg, 2002.

Rempel, David. "The Expropriation of the German Colonists in South Russia during the Great War." *Journal of Modern History* vol. IV (1932): 49–67.

Ripets'kyi, Stepan. *Ukrains'ke Sichove strilets'tvo. Vyzvol'na ideia i zbroinyi chyn*. New York: Vyd. "Chervona Kalyna," 1956.

Rothenberg, G. E. *The Army of Francis Joseph* (West Lafayette, IN: Purdue University Press, 1976).

Rudnytsky, Ivan L. "The Ukrainians in Galicia under Austrian Rule." In Ivan L. Rudnytsky, *Essays in Modern History*, pp. 315–352. Edmonton, AB: Canadian Institute of Ukrainian Studies, 1987).

Shavel'skii, Georgii. *Vospominaniia poslednego protopresvitera rossiiskoi armii i flota*. New York, 1954.

Skoropads'kyi, Pavlo. *Spohady: kinets' 1917-hruden' 1918*, ed. Jaroslaw Pelenski. Kyiv/Philadelphia: National Academy of Sciences of Ukraine, M. S. Hrushevs'kyi Institute of Ukrainian Archeography and Fontology, V. K. Lypynsky East European Research Institute, 1995.

Stojko, Wolodymyr. "Ukrainian National Aspirations and the Russian Provisional Government." In Taras Hunczak, ed., *The Ukraine, 1917–1921: A Study in Revolution*, pp. 4–32. Cambridge, MA: Harvard Ukrainian Research Institute, 1977.

Stone, Norman. *The Eastern Front 1914–1917*. New York: Charles Scribner's Sons, 1975.

Sumskii, S. "Odinnadtsat' perevorotov," edited by S. A. Alekseev. *Revoliutsiia na Ukraine*. Moscow and Leningrad: Gosudarstvennoe izdatel'stvo, 1930.

Szporluk, Roman. *The Political Thought of Thomas G. Masaryk*. New York: Columbia University Press, 1981.

Szporluk, Roman. Review of *The Ukraine, 1917–1921*, by T. Hunczak, ed. *Annals of the Ukrainian Academy of Arts and Sciences in the United States* 14 (1978–80): 268.

Szuber, Antoni. *Walka o przewage duchowa. Kampanja propagandowa koalicji 1914–1918*. Warsaw, 1933.

Thimme, Hans. *Weltkrieg ohne Waffen*. Stuttgart and Berlin: Cotta, 1932.

Tiander, Karl. *Das Erwachen Osteuropas. Die Nationalitaetenbewegung in Russland und der Weltkrieg*. Wien-Leipzig: Wilhelm Braumueller, 1934.

Torke, Joachim, and John-Paul Himka, eds., *German-Ukrainian Relations in Historical Perspective*. Edmonton and Toronto, ON: Canadian Institute of Ukrainian Studies Press, 1994.

Tsereteli, I. G. *Vospominaniia o fevral'skoi revoliutsii*. 2 vols. Paris: Mouton & Co., 1963.

von Hagen, Mark. "I Love Russia, but Want Ukraine: How a Russian Imperial General Became Hetman Pavlo Skoropadsky of the Ukrainian State." In Frank Sysyn and Serhii Plokhii, eds., *Synopsis: A Collection of Essays in Honor of Zenon E. Kohuti*. Edmonton and Toronto, ON: Canadian Institute of Ukrainian Studies Press, 2005.

von Hutten-Czapski, Bogdan. *60 Jahre Politik und Gesellschaft*, 2 Bde. Berlin: E. S. Mittler, 1936.

Vulpius, Ricarda. *Nationalisierung der Religion: Russifizierungspolitik und ukrainische Nationsbildung 1860–1920*. Wiesbaden: Harrassowitz Verlag, 2005.

Vyynychenko, V. *Vidrodzhennia natsii*, Vol. I. Kiev-Vienna: Vyd. Dzvin, 1920.

Wendland, Anna Veronika. *Die Russophilen in Galizien Ukrainische Konservative zwischen Oesterreich und Russland 1848–1915*. Wien: Verlag der Österreichischen Akademie der Wissenschaften, 2001.

Wheeler-Bennett, John. *Brest-Litovsk: The Forgotten Peace*, March 1918. London: Macmillan, 1938.

Winter, Eduard. *Byzanz und Rom im Kampf um die Ukraine, 955–1939*. Leipzig: Otto Harrassowitz, 1942.

Zeman, Z. *Germany and the Revolution in Russia*. London: Oxford University Press, 1958.

Zetterberg, Seppo. *Die Liga der Fremdvoelker Russlands 1916–1918. Ein Beitrag zu Deutschlands antirussischen Propagandakrieg unter den Fremdvoelkern Russlands im ersten Weltkrieg*. Helsinki: Finnish Historical Society, 1978.

Ingram Content Group UK Ltd.
Milton Keynes UK
UKHW010643220323
418970UK00006B/434